Quad Cities
An American Mosaic

Roald Tweet

East Hall Press

Quad Cities

An American Mosaic

For Margaret, who never backs down

The Quad Cities: An American Mosaic is a project sponsored by the Quad City Heritage League. The League is an Iowa-chartered not-for-profit corporation whose purpose is to promote interest in and understanding of the history and heritage of the Quad Cities.

Acknowledgements:

The Quad City Heritage League extends special thanks to the many people and organizations who helped make *The Quad Cities: An American Mosaic*, a reality.

> Michael J. Smith, first president of the League and former Director of the Putnam Museum of History and Natural Science, Davenport, initiated the project and guided much of its progress. He had the vision of a history book that treated the Quad Cities as a single community with a common and integrated past.

> Roald Tweet, the author, planned researched, wrote, edited and rewrote the text.

> Marlene Gantt conducted the historical research on the local firms.

> Sam Whitehead gathered the photographs to accompany the text.

> Students of East Hall Press, Augustana College, designed the page layouts and formatted the text electronically.

Printed by The Brandt Company, Davenport, IA

About the Author:

Roald D. Tweet is an educator and writer with a long-term interest in the Quad-Cities area. He has taught at Augustana College Rock Island. since 1960. where he is a Professor of English.
In addition to his distinguished academic career Dr Tweet has written extensively on subjects of local interest. Among his published works are: *History of Transportation on the Upper Mississippi and Illinois Rivers* and *History of the Rock Island District Corps of Engineers*. He was also a contributor to *Quad Cities: Joined by a River* and has served as a consultant on regional exhibits for the Putnam Museum of History and Natural Science in Davenport.
Dr. Tweet holds a masters degree in English and a Ph.D. in American Literature from the University of Chicago.

A Table of Contents

Foreward

Daniel Elazar in his book *The American Mosaic* notes, "All human groups are located in a particular space, in a particular time, and in a particular culture. . . . Each location is shaped by the deposits of people and cultures who settle it and by the varying ways in which they use the land over time." The locations "can be seen as resting on earlier locational 'strata' which in turn continue to influence contemporary life. . . . What is notable about the U.S. is the diversity of geo-historical locations resulting from the varieties of geographies, peoples, cultures and settlement periods with the nation."

This book is about one part of that mosaic: the Quad Cities, a metropolitan area which straddles the Mississippi River in western Illinois and eastern Iowa. It is a particular place with a unique history and identity which, at the same time, reveals historical patterns and processes characteristic of many other Midwestern cities. Professor Tweet describes the Quad Cities as "decidedly an American mosaic—an encyclopedia of 19th Century American settlement patterns which sprinkled the landscape of the Midwest with villages and towns. Here is the mill town, the river town, the paper city, the county seat, the crossroads village, the railroad town, the mining community, the military reservation, the factory town and the planned city."

What are the Quad Cities, the common reference to this metropolitan area? The three largest cities are Davenport, Iowa, and Rock Island and Moline, Illinois, causing the area to be called Tri-Cities for many years. Then, as East Moline, Illinois, and later Bettendorf, Iowa, sought inclusion in the regional name, the term Quad Cities emerged with the inevitable confusion of which one is the fourth city. In reality the metropolitan area should be called Quint Cities, but it has never caught on as a place name. In 1972 Rand McNally began to use "Quad Cities" on some of its maps. Another definition of the Quad Cities is the area within the quadrangle formed by the major interstate highways, I-80 and I-280, surrounding the urban area which would include all or part of nine additional small towns.

However one defines the Quad-Cities, Professor Tweet notes that on a map these cities, towns and villages resemble a mosaic. Each community has its own history, its own boosters and villains. Each tells its own stories. Yet, like a mosaic, no community stands alone. A network of roads and the complexities of modern life have woven the pieces of ceramic into a whole.

The Mississippi River's function as a municipal, county and state boundary is a major contributor to the cities' settlement fragmentation and mosaic quality. This arrangement was set by the Treaty of 1763 which, at the end of the so-called Seven Years War between the British and the French, divided the interior territory of America with the French west of the Mississippi and the British to the east. Two decades later the Old Northwest territory became part of the United States and soon it was subdivided into territories and eventually states, including Illinois in 1818. The section west of the Mississippi did not become part of America until after the 1803 Louisiana Purchase. The subdivision of that vast area into territories and states followed its own timetable including Iowa becoming a state in 1846.

This time differential bestowed upon the Quad Cities region a set of political divisions which have been significant in the historical development of a unique place. Today it is the one major metropolitan area in the country which is bi-state in character with approximately equal numbers of people on both sides of the boundary. Beginning with the creation of the predecessor of the Bi-State Regional Commission in the 1960s, many civic leaders have sought to find ways to overcome the boundary effect of this river, most notably under the "joined by the river" theme of the early 1980s. The irregularity with which the calls for unity and cooperation have been received by both leaders and common citizens is evident almost daily in the political, cultural and economic life of this place.

Professor Tweet also notes the human mosaic of this place as derived from the sequence of settlement and from various ethnicities, religions, occupations, abilities, and interests. They came from everywhere, "an encyclopedia of American types. Here is the fur trader, the visionary, the inventory, the tinkerer, the entrepreneur, the crime boss, the speculator, the solid citizen, the educator, the migrant, the laborer and the corporate leader."

This book is a history of this place with its mosaic quality. It comes to us at a time when there is increasing interest among scholars from many disciplines as well as local residents in the uniqueness and importance of place and of good local history. For example, the National Geography Standards 1994 entitled *Geography for Life* suggests that "place" is one of the five main themes of geographic understanding. The character of any place begins with "the relationships between physical environmental characteristics, such as climate, topography and vegetation, and such human characteristics as economic activity, settlement and land use. Together, these characteristics make each particular place meaningful and special to people. . . . . Our sense of self is intimately entwined with that of place. Places are parts of Earth's space, large or small, that have been endowed with meaning by humans." But there is more at stake, including personal identity and community identity. Local residents everywhere through individual or collective acts reveal a concern for place identity. They hope that their town or city, regardless of where it is and how large it is, will have a desirable "place on the map." The signs welcoming visitors to many towns and cities in a region give tangible evidence of the historical and contemporary quest for place identity, proclaiming that the town is the capital of this or the gateway to that or the heart of a special region or the home of a famous person or the largest whatever.

The Quad Cities region is such a "place." From the natural landscape encountered and used by Native Americans to the region discovered for the first time by the European explorers Marquette and Joliet in 1673 to the years of permanent settlement, the area has had a special quality to visitors and to inhabitants. A nineteenth century writer Henry Lewis describes the promise of these lands.

> No person can pass down the Mississippi and view the immense bodies of uncultivated
> lands, lying contiguous to its banks, without reflecting on the great changes which time will
> produce. . . . We can comprehend the great destiny, awaiting only the development of time, in
> store for this already far-farmed region.

From these beginnings the Quad-Cities has sought and achieved various identities, frequently focusing on its "river city" character or its agricultural role as the Farm Implement Capital of the World, but also revealing other qualities. Professor Roald Tweet in this book describes the dynamic physical geographic setting of this place and some of the major historical events and processes and people who settled and developed this land. Drawing upon official documents, a rich variety of archival materials, his own experiences as a resident and scholar of this region and the written and oral traditions shared by many Quad Citians from their backgrounds, he shows how this mix of physical and cultural relationships has given this place a unique story which needs to be told, heard, appreciated, and enhanced in our individual and collective contemporary lives in this region.

While being a unique place with its particular history, the Quad Cities' history also has enough similarities with other cities in this midwestern region to fit into the special category of "cities of the heartland." In this context the preparation of this book shortly after the 1993 publication of Jon Teaford's *Cities of the Heartland: The Rise and Fall of the Industrial Midwest* is a fortunate coincidence. Like Tweet, Teaford describes heartland cities "not as monoliths but as mosaics." He characterizes the Old Northwest as "a region whose cities possessed certain social, political, economic, cultural and ethnic characteristics that distinguished them as a class apart from the other metropolises in the nation." These cities usually shared the common origins of location on major waterways, the linkages to railroad developments in the mid-nineteenth century, the extraction of raw materials for the fabrication of metal products and other manufacturing, the processing of grain and livestock from the surrounding rich soils, and the fabrication of farm implements and construction of wagons for the millions of agrarian consumers in the region. Moreover, they "became home to people of diverse ethnic backgrounds and of every social and economic status. Rich and **poor,** black and white, German and Pole, all sought their fortunes in these hubs." His generalizations frequently seem as if the Quad Cities were the specific place he had in mind which will become more evident as you read this book.

Teaford also presents a case for a "distinctive heritage" and "a common **heartland** consciousness" in Midwestern cities. In the nineteenth century they were "cultural ports where cargoes of those valued commodities known as civilization and refinement regularly disembarked," places which through their connections could overcome the isolation of the midcontinent." Professor Tweet in his volume repeats this theme when he notes: "Town builders shared a common vision: to bring civilization, not to get away from it." By the early years of the twentieth century the Midwest was seen as central to the industrial and commercial life of America. Culturally and politically, the region and its cities came to be seen as "the nation's most typically American area." Again, this theme is echoed by Tweet: at the end of the 19th century, Tri-Citians (which was the common reference when there were only three large cities) looked back with satisfaction on their progress and forward with anticipation to the new century. Like an Horatio Alger hero, the Tri-Cities had "made something of themselves in this world."

In the last half of this century most of these cities have suffered through the economic decline caused by the decentralization of wealth and have been tagged with the label of "rust-belt cities." Teaford concludes that "metropolises of the heartland are a product of a region that has traditionally claimed to be the American norm but is in fact a distinguishable fragment of the national whole. There is, then, merit in examining the midwestern city as a distinctive phenomenon. It is a legitimate subspecies of urban life." Despite the seemingly good fit of the Quad Cities with these themes, for unknown reasons he makes no references to any of the cities which comprise this Quad Cities metropolitan area. Thus, it is timely that this volume now presents an overview of some of the major historical events and processes, including up to the current decade, of this region which enable it to be used as one more example of a "heartland city."

In conclusion, being unique and yet sharing common historical and cultural themes with other places, the Quad Cities is both a mosaic in its own make-up and a part of the broader mosaic that is the American landscape. To study this place through books like this one offers pleasant rewards for both local residents and Midwestern scholars. I believe others will join me in expressing appreciation to Professor Tweet and the Quad City Heritage League for preparing and presenting this volume.

Norman Moline
Professor of Geography
Augustana College

CHAPTER ONE:

Setting the Stage

On May 10, 1823, at about noon, a small sternwheel steamboat drew within sight of Fort Armstrong at the tip of a high rock island in the Upper Mississippi River amid a welcoming salute of cannon from the fort and musket fire from Sauk and Mesquakie Indians along the shore. Although she was little more than a flatboat, 118 feet long and 18 feet wide, a steam engine sitting open on the deck, with no pilot house and only a roofed cargo box at the rear for passengers and supplies, the *Virginia* had just made history. She was the first steamboat to cross the Des Moines Rapids above Keokuk and come this far upriver.

The *Virginia* carried passengers and military supplies bound for Fort St. Anthony (later re-named Fort Snelling) near present-day St. Paul, Minnesota. Among the passengers on board was the Italian world traveler, Count Giacomo Beltrami, who found himself among a cross-section of frontier types: Lawrence Taliaferro, the Indian Agent at Ft. St. Anthony, along with soldiers, settlers, a missionary lady going to preach to the Indians, boatmen, and Great Eagle, a Sauk Chief who had been to St. Louis to confer with General William Clark (of Lewis and Clark fame). Beltrami reported that Great Eagle quickly took off the uniform Clark had given him and continued the trip "in *status quo* of our first parents."

Upstream from Fort Armstrong, the *Virginia* faced a stretch of rapids more treacherous than those at Keokuk. To increase the chances of crossing the rapids, the *Virginia* took on as pilot George Davenport, a former provisioner for troops at the fort and now an Indian trader living on the island. Davenport was familiar with the rapids, but still, the boat stuck fast on a rock, and might have remained there had not "Providence come to our aid and swelled the waters of the river for two days." After resting at the head of the rapids following the three-day ordeal, the *Virginia* continued on to Fort Saint Anthony.

Captain John Crawford and his passengers knew they were making history by crossing the rapids. On the Lower Mississippi below St. Louis, the steamboat had already developed a lively trade in the decade since its arrival in 1812. Above St. Louis, however, the two

rapids and a shallow, sandbar-filled channel limited traffic to flatboats, keelboats, and canoes, good for hauling furs and lead from the mines at Galena, but unsuitable for settling whole towns.

As a result, Illinois became a state in 1818 solely by settling its southern half. The tide of immigration waited impatiently to move north into the rich tallgrass prairies stretching in all directions from Fort Armstrong, land which one contemporary immigrant guide book called the most fertile anywhere on earth, where "every rood [1/4 acre] may support its man," and raw materials for manufacture lay so abundant that coal "costs less to quarry than to chop wood."

The *Virginia* opened the way. On board, Beltrami met a family from Kentucky headed for the lead mines at Galena "with their arms and baggage, cats and dogs, hens and turkeys and children." He was amazed by the American citizens' "spirit of speculation," but even he could not have imagined the speed with which the region around Fort

COUNT GIACOMO BELTRAMI, THE ITALIAN WORLD TRAVELER, WAS A PASSENGER ON THE VIRGINIA, THE FIRST STEAMBOAT TO CROSS THE DES MOINES RAPIDS ON THE MISSISSIPPI AND COME THIS FAR UPRIVER. BELTRAMI AND THE VIRGINIA PASSED FORT ARMSTRONG ON MAY 10, 1823.

Courtesy, Augustana College Library, Special Collections

Armstrong would be settled by these restless Americans. Captain W. L. Clark, son of the founder of Buffalo, Iowa, could later brag that he had "lived in the Territory of Michigan, the Territory of Wisconsin, the Territory of Minnesota, Black Hawk's Purchase, Iowa Territory, and the State of Iowa, and only moved one mile." Had Beltrami taken this same trip just twenty years later, he could have landed at thriving communities on either shore of the river near Fort Armstrong, found a good hotel room for the night, read from a choice of local newspapers, attended the church of his choice, or entertained himself by taking in a lecture at the Davenport lyceum on "Is mind material—Or, can mind exist independent of matter?"

From the many settlements springing up around sawmills, flourmills, ferry landings, and steamboat stops would grow a metropolitan center of nearly 400,000 people. The Twin Cities of the 1830s would become the Tri-Cities by the Civil War, and the Quad Cities by the end of World War II. The metropolitan area that began with Rock Island and Davenport now comprises eleven contiguous communities, the center of a larger area covering two states, three counties, with 47 municipalities, 55 township governments, 30 school districts, and a total of 223 separate government entities.

On a map, these cities, towns, and villages resemble a mosaic. Each community has its own history, its own boosters and villains. Each tells its own stories. Yet, like a mosaic, no community stands alone. A network of roads, and the complexities of modern life have woven the pieces of ceramic into a whole. This history is the story of that mosaic.

It is, decidedly, an American mosaic—an encyclopedia of 19th century American settlement patterns which sprinkled the landscape of the Midwest with villages and towns. Here is the mill town, the river town, the paper city, the county seat, the crossroads village, the railroad town, the mining community, the military reservation, the factory town, and the planned city.

The cast of characters, those who came to settle and work here, reads like an encyclopedia of American types. Here is the fur trader, the visionary, the inventor, the tinkerer, the entrepreneur, the crime boss, the speculator, the solid citizen, the educator, the migrant, the laborer, and the corporate leader. They came from everywhere, second and third generation Americans from the upland South and New England, followed by Germans, Irish, Swedes, Hungarians and Jews, and then blacks, Hispanics, Greeks, and Belgians, down to our recent immigrants from southeast Asia. Each group, in turn, has found in the Quad Cities, a new frontier.

Ancient Seas and Glaciers

During the Devonian Period of the Paleozoic Era, some 300 million years in the past, a shallow sea covered much of central North America. Over millions of years, bones and shells of fishes and invertebrates collected on the sea floor, setting the stage for the drama of the Quad Cities. Under time and pressure, these skeletons became Devonian limestone, the bedrock of the entire Quad Cities region.. This layer became the island on which Fort

Armstrong sat, and the limestone quarries at LeClaire, Iowa, and Milan, Illinois, which provided the stone for many Quad Cities buildings.

During the Pennsylvanian Period, 285 million years ago, the seas gave way to swamps and marshes filled with prehistoric trees and giant ferns. Their decaying vegetation became coal—a three-to-six-foot vein under much of the Quad Cities.

Then, about a million years ago, during the Pleistocene Epoch, four major glaciers shaped and reshaped northern Illinois and Iowa. The glaciers left debris—sand, clay, gravel, and silt—thirty to sixty feet deep in Iowa and Illinois. Above that, wind-blown loess covered the region with fifteen to thirty feet of rich soil for future farms. Runoff from the glaciers created rivers and tributaries which eventually eroded deep channels, giving the Upper Mississippi Valley the steep bluffs that reminded early European visitors of the Rhine Valley.

It was the very last of these glaciers some eighteen thousand years ago that formed the Rock Island Rapids—by far the youngest stretch of the entire Mississippi River. Earlier glaciers had pushed the Mississippi into its present channel from Clinton, Iowa, north, but from there they sent the channel first into central Illinois, and then into Iowa. Only in the last ice age did the Iowa and Tazwell glaciers meet near Clinton and force the Mississippi into its present channel through the Quad Cities. Here the river was forced to turn west for fifteen miles across a hard limestone outcropping before meeting an older channel again at Muscatine, Iowa. That outcropping, just beginning to wear down, became the Rock Island Rapids. Here the Mississippi is also at its narrowest, its channel divided by a large rock island, making it a natural point to cross the river, an ideal source for water power, and therefore an almost inevitable site for urban development.

Actors Arrive

The retreating curtain of the last glaciers was the signal for life to make its entrance. By about 10,000 B.C. Paleo-Indians, the Big Game Hunters, followed the mastodon and mammoth to the Mississippi Valley. As these large animals disappeared around 8,000 B.C., the hunters and gatherers settled into small, semi-permanent communities.

This Woodland Culture reached its height between 500 B.C. and 1,000 A.D. in the Quad Cities region. Indians of the Eastern Woodland Tradition lived in mat or bark-covered lodges holding several families. They grew corn, squash, sunflowers, and perhaps beans. Evidence of this culture exists today in the Mississippi Valley in the form of burial and ceremonial mounds, several of which can be seen in Black Hawk State Park in Rock Island.

By about 1,400 A.D., the Woodland Culture gave way in eastern Iowa and northern Illinois to the Oneota Culture, ancestors of the Missouri, Oto and Ioway, Siouan-speaking tribes who first made contact with European explorers and traders. East of the Mississippi, by historic times, lived a loose federation of Algonquian-speaking tribes known as the Illiniwek (changed by the French to Illinois).

The two tribes most closely identified with the Quad Cities, the Sauk and the Mesquakie, were latecomers. Like other Algonquin tribes, they were pushed further and further west from their ancestral home in eastern Canada by the Iroquois. The Sauk (people of the yellow earth) and Mesquakie (people of the red earth) were related, but maintained separate villages.

By 1660 in their move west, the Sauk and Mesquakie reached Green Bay, Wisconsin, and soon controlled large areas of land along the Wisconsin River and along the Fox River in northern Illinois. Sometime after 1700 the Sauk moved down the Rock River to its mouth at the Mississippi and built their principle village, Saukenuk, in about 1730. The village was only semi-permanent, but by the time Europeans came to stay in 1816, Saukenuk was located at the mouth of the Rock River near where present-day 11th Street and Black Hawk road meet in Rock Island.

Saukenuk redefined the image of Native Americans for many visitors. It was home to at least three thousand Sauk, laid out at right angles with the point—location of the chief's lodge—facing the river. From the point, avenues stretched out along each

angle with lodges on both sides and alleys behind. The largest avenue—main street—was used for military drills, games and social gatherings. The lodges themselves were multiple family dwellings made of arched saplings and logs covered with bark or mats. Contemporary reports put the number of lodges at between 60 and 100. Outside the village lay fenced pasture for horses and as much as 800 acres of corn fields and gardens for beans, melons, and squash.

Meanwhile, the Mesquakie in eastern Illinois ran into trouble with French traders by charging tolls for the use of "their" streams. It was the French who named them the Renard, or "Fox," Indians, a name that became more common than Mesquakie. The French eventually fought back and, allied with several Illinois tribes, determined to drive the Mesquakie out of Illinois. On September 8, 1730, near Starved Rock, Illinois, between 1,000 and 1,200 Mesquakie men, women, and children were massacred. The remnant sought protection of their Sauk relatives at the Rock River. They settled in small villages along both sides of the Mississippi, including the present sites of Rock Island and Davenport.

The Sauk and Mesquakie were soon drawn into European conflicts. On June 17, 1673, Father Marquette and the explorer Louis Joliet reached the mouth of the Wisconsin River and become the first white men to discover the Upper Mississippi River. Marquette and Joliet claimed no territory, but they were followed by others who did. By 1713, the French empire extended from Quebec to the Gulf of Mexico.

Meanwhile, British colonists were already expanding west of the Allegheny Mountains. This, and competition for fur led to the French and Indian

Courtesy, Augustana College Library, Special Collections

THE PRINCIPLE VILLAGE OF THE SAUK INDIANS WAS SAUKENUK. THE VILLAGE WAS LOCATED ALONG THE ROCK RIVER NEAR ITS MOUTH AT THE MISSISSIPPI. THIS PAINTING WAS DONE BY PROFESSOR OLAF GRAFSTROM, ONE-TIME HEAD OF THE ART DEPARTMENT AT AUGUSTANA COLLEGE.

War in 1756, and to the Seven Years' War in Europe. At its close, the Treaty of Paris in 1763 gave England control of French lands east of the Mississippi.

Even as traders from the Hudson Bay Company set up an extensive network of posts to trade furs, England was having trouble with her own colonies. When trouble turned to rebellion in 1776, the Sauk and Mesquakie were forced to take sides. They had developed good trade relations with the English, who gave them gifts and credit; at the same time, they respected the power of the Americans. Finally, in 1780, they joined a force of British soldiers and Peoria Indians in attacking the Spanish fort at St. Louis. In retaliation, General George Rogers Clark, commanding American forces in the west, sent Colonel John Montgomery and a force of 250 men to destroy Indian villages along the Illinois River. Montgomery continued on to the Rock River where he burned Saukenuk in the westernmost encounter of the Revolutionary War.

The Treaty of Paris in 1783 brought the United States all the British lands east of the Mississippi and south of the Great Lakes. As part of this treaty, the British, loyal to their Indian allies, insisted that the new lands be "subject to Indian occupancy," to which the Americans reluctantly agreed.

Twenty years later, Americans owned the west bank of the Mississippi, too. President Jefferson had sought to buy land at the mouth of the Mississippi to protect American shipping, but eagerly accepted Napoleon's counter offer to sell all of Louisiana Territory for 15 million dollars. On April 30, 1803, the United States and France signed the Louisiana Purchase Treaty. The entire Quad Cities region was now American.

American ownership meant trouble for the Sauk and Mesquakie. The French, Spanish, and English had only been interested in trade with the Indians. The Americans wanted the land itself. In 1804, four Sauk Indians from the Des Moines Rapids area, in St. Louis to obtain the release of a tribal member held for murder, found themselves signing a treaty arranged by William Henry Harrison, Governor of Indiana Territory and the District of Louisiana (the north half of the Louisiana Purchase), in which they relinquished all rights to Sauk and Mesquakie lands east of the Mississippi and west of the Mississippi to the watersheds of the Des Moines. In return for swearing allegiance to the United States alone, the treaty promised that the government would "never interrupt the said tribes in the possession of lands which they rightfully claim" so long as the government owned the land.

The Sauk and Mesquakie were again caught between the Americans and the English. They continued their annual pilgrimages to Fort Malden in Amherstburg, Canada, across from Detroit, where resistance to the Americans was encouraged.

Conflicts between American and British fur companies helped precipitate the War of 1812. Caught in the middle, the Sauk and Mesquakie divided. About 1,500 Indians, some sympathetic to the Americans and others anxious to avoid a fight, crossed the Mississippi into Missouri Territory and settled along the Des Moines River. From this Missouri band of Indians emerged a leader sympathetic to the Americans: Keokuk.

Some 200 Sauk warriors and their families chose to remain at Saukenuk. Their leader was Makataimeshekiakiak (Black Sparrow Hawk) who has come down in local legend as Chief Black Hawk, though he was a war leader rather than a chief. The Saukenuk group intended to remain neutral, but when the Americans defaulted on a promised load of provisions to see the Indians through the winter, and a British trader arrived with two boats full of supplies, Black Hawk, now 45, and his band enlisted on the British side.

At first, the war went well for the British who retook many northern posts. Then, in May of 1814, Missouri Governor William Clark retook Prairie du Chien. In July, to resupply this fort, three keelboats of reinforcements and supplies led by Lt. John Campbell were sent upriver from St. Louis. On the morning of July 19 as the boats were crossing the Rock Island Rapids, currents and a strong wind forced Campbell's boat aground on an underbrush-filled island which today bears his name. Lying in wait was an attack force of as many as 400 Sauk and Mesquakie, well armed by the British, opened fire point blank. Black Hawk himself set fire to Campbell's sail. One of the other boats eventually came to rescue the seriously wounded Campbell. Leaving the dead and dying, the American force then retreated to St. Louis. The Indians lost one man and one woman; the Americans, ten regulars, four rangers, a woman and a child. Twenty other Americans were wounded. The British later called this westernmost battle of the War of 1812 "the most brilliant victory of the war won by Indians unassisted by whites."

In August, to retaliate for Campbell's defeat, General Benjamin Howard, military commander at St. Louis, sent a fleet of eight keelboats and 430 men under Major Zachary Taylor to burn Saukenuk. Their surprise attack was discovered and they were forced to retreat to the Des Moines Rapids.

In 1816 Congress authorized a string of forts to protect American trade. On May 10, 1816, some 600 troops of the Eighth United States Infantry under Brevet Brigadier General Thomas A. Smith from Fort Independence at St. Louis landed on the island of Rock Island to build a fort named in honor of former Secretary of War, General John Armstrong. Lieutenant Zebulon Pike had recommended this site during an 1805 expedition because its high limestone cliffs rising thirty feet out of the water protected it from flood and attack, and because its location at the foot of the Rock Island Rapids allowed for the use of water power.

Before leaving construction of the fort in charge of Colonel William Lawrence, General Smith invited the Sauk and Mesquakie to a treaty council to confirm the 1804 treaty (even though building the fort itself was illegal according to that treaty). After refusing to attend for several days, Black Hawk and other leaders reluctantly met with General Smith on May 13 and signed.

Fort Armstrong was completed without incident and according to a standard plan for military posts. It was a square, 270 feet on each side, built at the very tip of the island. Two open sides of the fort were protected by the high cliff, while the two landside faces were protected by 8-foot stone walls supporting a breastwork of timbers five feet high. Two story wood block houses protected the three corners connected by walls.

Accompanying the troops to Rock Island was a private contractor, or sutler, hired to supply provisions to the fort, as was the custom at the time. George Davenport, his wife, Margaret Bowling Lewis, and a stepdaughter, Susan Lewis, built a double log cabin on the north shore several hundred yards from the fort to serve as a home and store. Here a year later, George L'Oste Davenport became the first white child born in the area.

George Davenport was born in Lincolnshire, England, in 1783. He came to the United States in 1804, and had become a sutler in 1815. Davenport's English background made him especially successful with the Sauk and Mesquakie, who called him Saganosh (Englishman).

In 1818 Davenport resigned his post as sutler to devote himself to Indian trade. He soon had outposts scattered across Iowa, Wisconsin,

KEOKUK WAS A SAUK AND MESQUAKIE INDIAN LEADER SYMPATHETIC TO THE AMERICANS DURING THE WAR OF 1812 WITH THE BRITISH. IN 1831, KEOKUK WAS APPOINTED "CHIEF OF THE SAUKS" BY THE UNITED STATES GOVERNMENT AFTER HE CAME TO FORT ARMSTRONG TO CONFIRM HIS OWN FRIENDSHIP WITH THE AMERICANS.

Courtesy, Augustana College Library, Special Collections

and Illinois, trading with many tribes.

Living across the river with relatives in a Mesquakie village was Antoine LeClaire, son of a French Canadian father and a Potawatomi mother. LeClaire had entered government service in 1812 at the request of Governor William Clark of Missouri, who sent him to school to learn English. He already spoke French and Spanish, in addition to fourteen Indian dialects. In 1816 LeClaire was hired by the commander of Fort Armstrong as an Indian Agent and interpreter. In 1820 LeClaire married Marguerite LePage, daughter of a Frenchman and granddaughter of the Sauk chief, Acoqua.

Indian Removal

Although Davenport and LeClaire were sympathetic to the Indians, there was little they could do to prevent the removal of the tribes from

THE ATTACK BY PRO-BRITISH SAUK AND MESQUAKIE INDIANS ON AMERICAN LIEUTENANT JOHN CAMPBELL OCCURED ON JULY 19, 1814 DURING THE WAR OF 1812. THE ISLAND WHERE THE AMBUSH TOOK PLACE WAS LATER NAMED IN HONOR OF CAMPBELL.

Courtesy, Augustana College Library, Special Collections

land desired by the Americans. On August 24, 1816, three months after Black Hawk had reconfirmed the Treaty of 1804, Governor Clark made a treaty with the Ottawas, Chippewas, and Potawatomi living along the Illinois River. In return for agreeing to leave their lands south of a boundary line due west from the tip of Lake Michigan, as well as land along the west shore of the lake (including the site of Chicago), these tribes were given the Sauk and Mesquakie lands along the Mississippi in Illinois.

The Indian Boundary Line was surveyed in 1819, and again in 1821, slightly askew, and forms the northern border of Lincoln Park in Rock Island and continues down 9th Avenue to the Mississippi. Saukenuk was south of this line, and temporarily safe.

Squatters soon appeared on Indian land. In 1824 George Davenport took a partner, Russell Farnham, in the fur trade. In 1826 this business became part of the American Fur Company, and the two men built a 2 1/2 story log cabin next to a Mesquakie village on the Illinois shore near the boat landing for Fort Armstrong. Known as the John Barrel House, this building served as hotel, trading post, tavern, and official polling place of the Rock Island Precinct of Jo Daviess County. That same year, Robert and Thomas Syms settled at the present site of Port Byron at the head of the rapids to provide wood to passing steamboats. By 1829, more than a hundred settlers had encroached on Indian land, and Saukenuk itself was being pressed.

Both Illinois and the United States now came to regret the terms of the 1804 treaty which permitted the Sauk and Mesquakie to remain on their lands "so long as it was owned by the United States." In 1829, George Davenport, in what appears to be a shift in

Courtesy, Putnam Museum

his sympathy for the Indians, requested that Saukenuk and all other Sauk and Mesquakie lands be surveyed, platted, and put up for sale. On October 19, 1829, at the Springfield land office, George Davenport and Russell Farnham bought nearly 80% of this Indian land, including the site of Saukenuk.

Earlier that same year, in the Treaty of July 29, 1829, the Government had repurchased the land north of the Indian Boundary Line from the three Illini tribes. As part of this treaty, tribal members who were part white were given some of the land. In this way, Antoine LeClaire and his brother Francois received two sections—1,280 acres—along the Indian Boundary Line where today Moline and East Moline stand.

Andrew Jackson's election as President in 1828 was a further blow for the Sauk and Mesquakie. Jackson's desire to send the Indians west ended with the Indian Removal Act of 1830. Davenport visited Jackson in 1830 to request that the Indians at least be paid for their lands rather than being forced off, but the request was denied, and the President "declared that they should move off."

Courtesy, Augustana College Library, Special Collections

Courtesy, Davenport Public Library

Anticipating the removal of the Indians, Illinois created Rock Island County out of the southern half of Jo Daviess County in 1831. By then, some 880 settlers were already there. That same spring, Black Hawk and his band returned from the winter hunt to find squatters living in Saukenuk itself, even occupying his own lodge. Fences had been pulled down and pasture plowed up. Fear of retaliation led the settlers to organize a paramilitary group calling themselves the Rock River Rangers. Among the 58 men who signed up were Joshua Vandruff, Rinnah Wells (and ten other Wells's), and John W. Spenser, who later became one of Rock Island's most distinguished citizens.

These rangers, together with elements of the state militia and six companies of United States infantry from St. Louis, confronted Black Hawk's band as they attempted to return to Saukenuk in June of 1831, and burned the village to the ground. The following day, under a white flag, Black Hawk surrendered. On June 30, he signed an "article of capitulation" promising to move permanently west of the Mississippi. During this confrontation, Keokuk had come to Fort Armstrong to confirm his own friendship. In return, the United States Government appointed him "Chief of the Sauks."

The Black Hawk War

Black Hawk spent the winter of 1831-32 trying to enlist other Sauk on his side, promising that both Illinois Indians and the British would join in resisting the Americans. Although he met with little success, on April 6, 1832, Black Hawk and some 1,000 followers—men, women, and children—crossed the river at Yellow Bank (Oquawka) and turned north toward the Rock River. George

Davenport sent a message to General Henry Atkinson at St. Louis informing him that "the British Band of Sac-Fox Indians is determined to make war on the frontier settlement . . . and commit depravations on the inhabitants of the frontier."

General Atkinson was already on his way with 220 men of the Sixth Infantry. Two companies of the First Infantry led by Lieutenant Colonel Zachary Taylor came down from Fort Crawford. On April 16, Governor Reynolds issued a call for volunteers. He also appointed George Davenport to the rank of Colonel, a title he kept from then on.

By early May, state and federal troops gathered on a farm owned by John Blazer at the junction of present-day Ridgewood and Andalusia Roads in Milan. Among the volunteers was a store clerk from New Salem, Abraham Lincoln, who was elected captain of his company, and two other future Civil War figures: Zachary Taylor and a young captain of the First Infantry, Jefferson Davis. Captain Davis later became the military escort for Black Hawk as he was taken to prison at Jefferson Barracks.

The Americans let Black Hawk reach the Rock River and head toward White Cloud's village before beginning pursuit. On May 9, 1832, an army of 2,000 foot soldiers and mounted troops began to track the Indians up the river. Aside from scattered violence against settlers and three "skirmishes," there was no war at all. For the next three months, as many as 3,700 troops under General Atkinson ineptly tracked a disheartened and hungry band of Sauks up the Rock into the Lake Koshkonong area of southeastern Wisconsin where the Indians turned back in retreat toward the Mississippi River.

On August 1, Black Hawk's band reached the Mississippi near the mouth of the Bad Axe River.

Courtesy, Augustana College Library, Special Collections

They were prevented from crossing the river by the steamboat *Warrior* returning to Fort Crawford, whose captain refused an offer to surrender and instead opened up with the boat's guns.

That night, Black Hawk and a small group of followers escaped toward the Wisconsin Dells region. The following day, the combined American troops forced the Sauk across a slough onto a small island. About 150 men, women, and children were killed by gunfire; others drowned trying to cross the river. A few Indians were taken prisoner. Only about 300 Sauk made it across the Mississippi to Iowa, where half of this remnant were killed by Wabasha and his Sioux warriors who had been waiting for them. Of the 1,000 Sauk who had crossed the river on April 6, fewer than 150 now remained alive. American casualties in the war were seventeen killed and twelve wounded.

Black Hawk was captured a week later and taken on a tour of eastern cities, including Washington, D.C., where President Jackson impressed him with the extent and power of the United States. Black Hawk understood. He wore the medal the President gave him, but he refused to sit for a portrait of himself with a spear in his hand.

In July of 1832, Atkinson was replaced as commander of the Army of the Frontier by General Winfield Scott, with orders to conclude a peace treaty. Because of a cholera outbreak at the fort, Scott held treaty negotiations on the Iowa side of the river near a Mesquakie encampment at what is now Farnam and 5th Street in Davenport. In the Treaty of September 21, 1832, between Governor Reynolds, General Scott, and Keokuk, the Sauk and Mesquakie ceded all their land in Illinois. In addition, they ceded a fifty-mile deep strip of land on the west bank of the Mississippi from the Yellow River south to the Des Moines, except for a reservation along the Iowa River where Keokuk's village stood. This tract of six million acres came to be known as the Black Hawk Purchase.

At the insistence of the Indians, Antoine LeClaire was given a section of land at the head of the rapids. Keokuk personally reserved a second section of land—the treaty site itself—for Marguerite LeClaire, whom the Indians especially admired for her many kindnesses toward them. Marguerite LeClaire's reserve ran between about Harrison and Bridge Avenues in present-day Davenport, and from the river almost to Locust Street. The only stipulation was that the LeClaires build a home on the very site where General Scott's marquee stood when he signed the treaty. This the LeClaires soon did.

In return for the surrender of their land, the Sauk and Mesquakie received $20,000 and forty kegs of tobacco a year. In addition, in order to "give a striking evidence of their mercy & liberality," the United States agreed to give the tribes 35 beef cattle, 12 bushels of salt, 30 barrels of pork and 50 of flour for the use of widows and children of Sauk killed in the war.

Black Hawk spent a year as a prisoner. On August 2, 1833, the anniversary of the Battle of Bad Axe, he was placed in Keokuk's custody. He lived with his wife and children along the Iowa River, and then the Des Moines. He died on October 3, 1838. Only an occasional arrowhead washed out by the rain, an annual Pow Wow by Mesquakie from Tama, a museum, and the name Black Hawk on plazas, parks, and businesses are left as reminders of the great community which flourished here for a hundred years.

POSTUMOUS PORTRAIT OF BLACK HAWK BY ISAAC WEATHERBY IN 1838. FOLLOWING HIS CAPTURE, BLACK HAWK WAS TAKEN ON A TOUR OF THE EAST COAST, INCLUDING A MEETING WITH PRESIDENT ANDREW JACKSON. AFTER ONE YEAR AS A PRISONER, BLACK HAWK WAS RELEASED. HE LIVED OUT HIS LAST FIVE YEARS IN IOWA.

Courtesy, Putnam Museum

(RIGHT PAGE) IN 1832, BEFORE IOWA WAS OPENED FOR SETTLEMENT, GEORGE L. DAVENPORT, THE COLONEL'S SON, CONSTRUCTED A HOUSE ON LAND HE CLAIMED ON PRESENT-DAY COLLEGE AVENUE IN DAVENPORT. THIS CLAIM HOUSE WAS PROBABLY THE FIRST FRAME HOUSE IN IOWA.

CLAIM HOUSE BUILT BY GEORGE L. DAVENPORT IN 1833.
AT 527 COLLEGE AVE DAVENPORT.

COURTESY, PUTNAM MUSEUM

CHAPTER TWO

Cities, Steamboats, and Railroads

EARLY IN 1833, CONGRESS RATIFIED GENERAL SCOTT'S TREATY WITH THE SAUK AND MESQUAKIE, AND APPOINTED JUNE 1 AS THE DATE FOR THEM TO vacate the Black Hawk Purchase. This date did not go unnoticed. Wide newspaper coverage of the Black Hawk War in the East and the South had attracted the attention of many second and third-generation Americans eager to move west for another chance at fame or fortune.

The land around Fort Armstrong seemed especially attractive. The fort lay due west from the tip of Lake Michigan in the direct path for settlers heading west. The narrow channel at the rapids, divided by the island, made this the easiest crossing point on the river. Settlers coming upriver from the Ohio would need help across the rapids. The transportation potential was enhanced by plentiful wood, limestone, and coal, and by almost unlimited water power from the 24-foot fall of the rapids.

Town builders shared a common vision: to bring civilization, not to get away from it, their towns shaped by eastern blueprints. Those who planned manufacturing towns–Moline, Camden, Rapids City–

imagined "the Lowell of the Mississippi," while the builders of river ports such as Davenport and Stephenson fancied they were platting "embryo Cincinnatis." With Chicago still a newly incorporated village in 1833, every settlement was free to dream of becoming the "Queen City" of the Midwest.

Anticipating this shift from frontier to civilization, Colonel George Davenport in 1833 replaced his log cabin and trading post with an imposing two-story clapboard-covered log frame house on the north shore of the island. For the next twelve years, Davenport hosted here an unofficial chamber of commerce where towns were projected and laid out, new businesses planned, investors talked into settling, and a railroad born. The Davenport House became what one historian has called "the cradle of the Quad Cities."

Had it not been for the Davenports, and for Antoine and Marguerite LeClaire across the river, the settlement of the Quad Cities would have been neither so successful nor so rapid. Their concern for the towns they founded, their generosity and encouragement of churches and schools, and their support of settlers helped give birth to the Quad Cities.

Stakes and Towns

Within seven years after the opening of the Black Hawk Purchase, more than twenty towns appeared along both sides of the Mississippi, springing up around wood supplies, mills, and stage stops. By 1836, town builders at four separate locations along the river believed they had found the ideal site;

FERRIES LIKE THIS ONE WERE IN BUSINESS FOR MANY YEARS ON THE MISSISSIPPI AND ROCK RIVERS. H.L. ANGELL'S FERRY, PICTURED HERE, ON THE ROCK RIVER WAS ESTABLISHED IN 1854 AND CONTINUED TO RUN UNTIL ABOUT 1915.

Courtesy, Rock Island County Historical Society.

at each of these four sites, rival towns appeared across the river from each other.

Early in 1833, Captain Benjamin W. Clark established a ferry service ten miles downstream from Farnhamsburg, and waited for the first settlers to cross into the Black Hawk Purchase. Clark believed that the four separate channels at the mouth of the Rock River, would discourage immigrants from crossing north to use George Davenport's ferry. Then, realizing that westward-bound immigrants would provision themselves on the Iowa rather than the Illinois side, he moved across the river to his Iowa ferry landing, opened a public house, and in May of 1836, laid out Buffalo, the first town platted in what would soon (1838) become Scott County.

Captain Clark sold his Illinois site in 1836 to speculators who platted a large town called Rockport. They sold thousands of dollars of lots to prominent individuals back East but Rockport was never built. In 1843, a Rock Island businessman, Napoleon Buford, bought Rockport at a tax sale. In 1845, his wife named this new town Andalusia.

Two years after Clark settled at Buffalo, an Ohioan, Captain John Sullivan, and several others, founded Rockingham several miles upstream, directly across the Mississippi from the mouth of the Rock River. The State of Illinois was working on a canal around the rapids at the mouth of the Rock River in order to open northern Illinois, and even the Great Lakes, to the Mississippi. Although the Rockingham site was not ideal—it turned into an island in high water—the possibility of controlling such a lucrative market made wet ground easy to overlook. Sullivan platted Rockingham in the summer of 1836. By that winter there were 13 houses and a hundred people— twice the size of Davenport five miles east.

Across from Rockingham on the site of Saukenuk, a group of investors laid out Rock Island City, to take advantage both of the expected trade from the Rock River, and of its water power. George Davenport sold them three-fourths of his 608-acre site at Saukenuk, retaining one-fourth for himself. Rock Island City was by far the grandest town of any on the Upper Mississippi, nearly ten times the size of Stephenson and Davenport. A prospectus described its 1,380 lots, the large brick buildings, the steamboat landings, and the busy streets, which existed only on paper. Among the many prominent Easterners who invested in this paper city was Daniel Webster, who eventually lost the $60,000 he invested.

Both Rockingham and Rock Island City might have done better had it not been for the Panic of 1837. Illinois, already overtaxed by extensive internal projects, abandoned plans for the canal. Rockingham survived and was absorbed into an expanding Davenport, but Rock Island City was declared vacated by the Illinois Legislature in 1837.

Two other urban sites developed at the head and foot of the Rock Island Rapids. Even in relatively high water, the growing number of steamboats traveling on the Upper Mississippi often had to transfer their cargo to small boats in order to cross the rapids. It was easy to predict in 1836 that the rapids would be an increasing obstacle to navigation, but it was difficult to predict whether boats would be more apt to stop at the rapids on their way upriver with supplies, or on the way down loaded with produce from new farms.

Antoine and Marguerite LeClaire did not have to choose. The Treaty of 1832 had given them a section of land at each end of the rapids. In 1835, LeClaire bought from two squatters a small piece of

Antoine LeClaire and George Davenport put up a hotel in Davenport in 1836. The Davenport House, as the hotel was called, was on the corner of Ripley and Front street (now River Drive). This photograph, taken in 1911, shows the Davenport House hotel seventy-five years after its completion.

Courtesy, Putnam Museum

land just west of his wife's reserve.. The following year, he formed an investment company of seven men, including George Davenport.

LeClaire named the town Davenport in honor of his friend. It was laid out in May of 1836 between present-day Harrison and Warren streets, and from the river to 7th Street, in thirty-six blocks and six half-blocks. Even though a steamboat full of speculators came up from St. Louis for the opening sale, investors were leary of the unclear title to the land, and only fifty or so lots out of 300 sold. Half a dozen families arrived in 1836. LeClaire and Davenport put up a hotel, the Davenport House, on the corner of Ripley and Front streets, but there were no businesses until late in the year. James McIntosh opened a small log cabin store in October, and in December, D. C. Eldridge opened a larger general store. The Panic of 1837 kept immigration low.

There was also competition across the river from the thriving town of Stephenson. In 1833 the Illinois Legislature completed plans for Rock Island County, ordering an election for county commissioners and a county government, and appointing a committee to select a site for a county seat. The Legislature specified that the new town be named Stephenson in honor of Colonel Benjamin Stephenson, who had played a small role in the Black Hawk War. Legislators hostile to George Davenport may have been trying to keep the town from being named Davenport.

In June of 1835, the committee recommended a 62-acre site along the river west of Farnhamsburg between present-day 10th and 17th streets in Rock Island. Stephenson was platted into twenty blocks with 80 by 150-foot lots worthy of a county seat. Even the alleys had names like Cherry, Peach, Violet, and Plum. Once its two-story brick courthouse was completed in 1837, citizens passed a housing code, as well as laws forbidding horse racing, gambling, and firecrackers (later amended to include "hallooing, shouting, bawling, screaming, obscene or profane language").

Stephenson's population reached 600 by 1840, with 175 houses, seven stores, three taverns, three groceries, four lawyers and three doctors. In 1841, residents petitioned the legislature to change the name to Rock Island. This new town included all the additions to Stephenson as well as the village of Farnhamsburg.

The sites at the head of the Rock Island Rapids were the last to be developed. In 1837, LeClaire completed plans for a town at the head of the rapids. Port Byron had been laid out the previous fall on the Illinois side, and a village named Parkhurst was developing next to the LeClaire Reserve. Both Parkhurst and LeClaire were laid out in the summer of 1837, separated by a small strip of dense forest known as "the Gulf."

Many additional towns were platted between these four locations. Cordova (1837), Hampton (1838) and Rapids City (1838) grew up between Stephenson and Port Byron. On the Iowa side, the possibility of the state capitol locating along the river led hopeful town builders in 1836 to stake out sites as close as a mile apart from Davenport downstream to present-day Muscatine. Below Davenport and Rockingham were Monte Video, Buffalo, Iowa, Montpelier, Salem, Wyoming, Geneva, Bloomington (Muscatine), and Newburgh. Few of these survived the Panic of 1837, which slowed immigration and curtailed the produce market.

By 1840, it was clear that the Twin Cities, Stephenson and Davenport, had chosen good locations and founders able to carry them through hard times. While many new villages struggled, these two grew into thriving frontier communities. Davenport's success was assured in 1840 after winning a heated series of contests with Rockingham for county seat. In spite of foul play on both sides (Davenporters imported several sleigh-loads of lead miners from Dubuque, "the most wretched looking rowdies that ever appeared on the streets of Davenport," and paid them ten barrels of whiskey to vote), the Rockingham faction graciously gave in to LeClaire's offer of a free Davenport site and $3,000 toward construction of the courthouse.

Davenport's population was only about half of Stephenson's 600 in 1840, but both towns could boast the beginnings of culture. Lyceums—"ladies welcome"—gave local citizens a chance to lecture and debate each other during the winter season. The demand for newspapers was met in 1838 when Andrew Logan brought the first steam press to Davenport and began publishing the weekly *Iowa Sun*. Stephenson's first papers, the *Rock Island Banner* and *Stephenson Gazette*, began the following year, and in 1840 the *Upper Mississippian* began publishing editions in both towns.

Churches were soon prominent in the townscapes. With land and a subsidy from LeClaire, a small Catholic congregation built St. Anthony's Church in 1838–for many years the largest building in town. Baptists, Methodists, and Congregationalists all built churches the following year. An Episcopal congregation which became Trinity was organized in 1841. In Stephenson, a Methodist Episcopal congregation in 1836 was followed by Presbyterians in 1841.

Antoine LeClaire built the LeClaire House hotel in 1839 on the corner of Second and Main Streets in Davenport. The hotel had a reading room on the ground floor which made availible more than forty of "the best newspapers in the country."

Cortesy, Putnam Museum.

Both towns offered a choice of private and parochial schools. Mariane Hall and the Reverend Michael Hummer opened a school for boys in Davenport in 1838, and the Misses O'Hara opened a "female seminary" the following year. By 1841, Stephenson (now Rock Island) could boast at least five private schools, including J. Alden Woodruff's Rock Island University (refusing admission to those who could not read) and D. J. Loyd's Select Academy (orthography, reading, writing, mental and practical arithmetic, botany, moral philosophy, and rhetoric).

Both communities could boast new hotels to host the growing number of visitors, the Rock Island House and the Island City Hotel (with its own theater) in Stephenson, and the LeClaire House on the corner of Second and Main in Davenport, where a reading room on the ground floor made available more

John W. Spencer was an early settler of the Tri-Cities. He was one of David B. Sears' partners in building the first dam across Sylvan Slough. These same partners were also involved in platting the town of Moline.

Courtesy, Augustana College Library, Special Collection.

than forty of "the best newspapers in the country."

Settling In

In 1836, David B. Sears and his family came from Cairo, Illinois, and settled near 15th Street in present-day Moline. At this point, the Island of Rock Island divided the Mississippi into a main channel to the north, and a smaller channel known as Sylvan Slough past the Illinois shore. Sometime between 1837 and 1841, Sears and two partners, Spencer H. White and John W. Spencer, began construction of a 600-foot dam across Sylvan Slough.

Sears built a mill on the Illinois side in 1838 which sawed wood, ground wheat and corn and carded wool. Sears' mill was so much faster and more dependable than earlier mills—twenty bushels of wheat an hour—that he soon had business from a wide area, including Iowa when wagons could cross the ice bridge in winter.

Sears and his partners had laid out a few lots south of his mill in 1841-2 as Rock Island Mills, but in 1843, they expanded their plans by buying a portion of the Huntington Wells farm east of the Rock Island Mills property, and platting the town of Moline.

The Sears Dam provided enough power for several mills and factories. In 1846, a New Englander, Charles Atkinson, built a sawmill ("the old red mill") on the dam itself. Spencer White built another sawmill on the island side. Next to the

John Deere was born in Rutland, Vermont, in 1804. He came to the Midwest in the mid-1830s and developed the self-scouring steel plow in 1837. Deere came to Moline in 1846 to take advantage of the Mississippi River's transportation and water power.

Courtesy, Rock Island Arsenal Museum.

White mill sat the Chamberlain & Dean sawmill, and a factory for making buckets and woodenware with power from the White mill. Next to the Sears Mill in Moline stood the Fergus and Buford Foundry. It was Colonel John Buford's offer of power from his waterwheel that brought the most important of all the users of the Sears Dam to Moline. In 1848, John Deere, the inventor of a self-scouring steel plow that eased the breaking of prairie sod on Midwest farms,

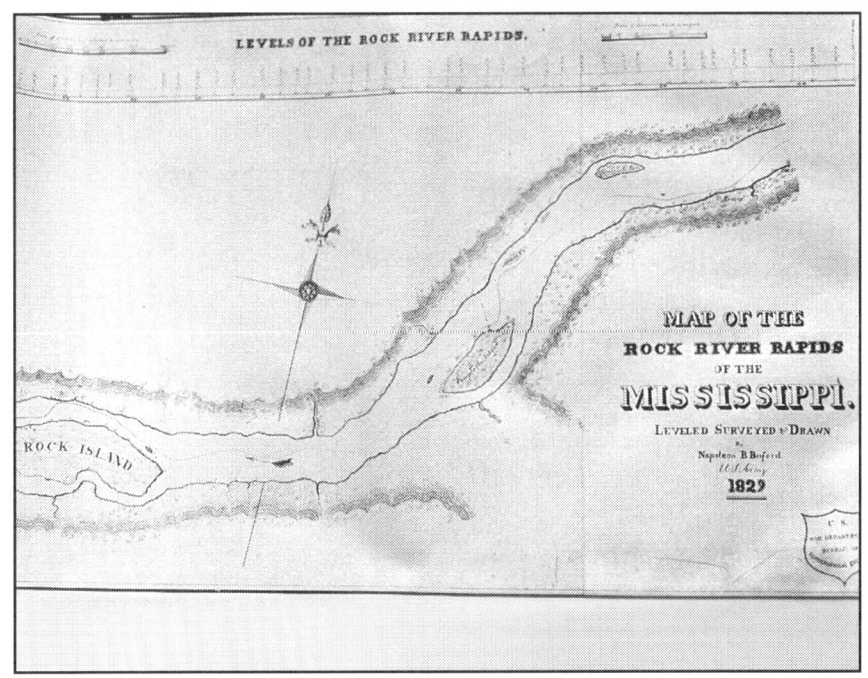

LEVELS OF THE ROCK RIVER RAPIDS.

MAP OF THE
ROCK RIVER RAPIDS
OF THE
MISSISSIPPI.
LEVELED SURVEYED & DRAWN
by
Napoleon B. Buford.
U.S. Army
1829

ROCK ISLAND

NAPOLEON BUFORD, THE SON OF COLONEL JOHN BUFORD, WAS A YOUNG LIEUTENANT SENT TO THE TRI-CITY AREA TO SURVEY THE ROCK ISLAND RAPIDS FOR THE TOPOGRAPHICAL BUREAU IN 1829. NINE YEARS LATER, NAPOLEON AND HIS THREE BROTHERS, ALONG WITH HIS FATHER, PERMANENTLY MOVED TO ROCK ISLAND FROM KENTUCKY.

Coutesy, Davenport Public Library.

moved his growing operations from Grand Detour, Illinois, to the Sears Dam. The arrival of Deere and his partner, Robert N. Tate, in the summer of 1848 soon turned Moline into "the Plow City."

As Moline grew around the Sears Mill, smaller operations were developing waterpower at the mouth of the Rock River. In 1843, William Dickson bought a claim south of the Rock River and laid out the town of Camden. On Vandruff's Island opposite Camden, other investors laid out the town of Lowell in 1844. A brush dam connecting Camden and Lowell powered grist and flour mills in both towns, so many, that the streets of Camden were often congested by teams hauling grain to the mills. As steam replaced waterpower, Lowell disappeared, but Camden survived, changing its name to Camden Mills in 1848, and to Milan in 1870.

As Moline was shaped by the visions of Deere, Sears, and Atkinson, Davenport and Rock Island benefitted from an influx of businessmen from the East and South with ideas and money. J. M. D. Burrows arrived in Davenport in 1838. He built a store and was soon shipping area farm produce to market. In 1843 he took his young clerk, R. M. Prettyman, as a partner in a number of ventures that helped establish Davenport's reputation as a commercial center.

The same year Burrows arrived in Davenport, Colonel John Buford left his family horse business in Kentucky and came to Rock Island with four sons, Napoleon, Thomas, John, and James. Napoleon had been here in 1829 as a

young lieutenant just out of West Point ordered to survey the Rock Island Rapids for the Topographical Bureau. Colonel Buford opened the first store on the Rock Island levee in 1838, with a square wooden front "gorgeously painted to look like granite." He boosted Rock Island whenever he could– "New Jerusalem," he called it–and accurately predict-ed that its population would one day be 50,000.

The Golden Age

On July 4, 1845, as his family celebrated the Fourth of July in Rock Island, Colonel George Davenport was murdered at his home by robbers. Although the six men involved were caught, and three of them, John and Aaron Long, and Granville Young were hung before a large public gathering in Rock Island, Davenport's murder reminded local citizens that they were not in such civilized country as their newspapers often claimed.

Nevertheless, Davenport's vision survived. 1845 was a year of looking ahead, too. In the next decade, a flood of immigrants from Europe and the rapid growth of steamboat traffic turned Davenport and Rock Island into fledgling commercial centers. Moline's growth was slower, but steady, and by the Civil War, the Twin Cities had become the Tri-Cities.

Much of that growth was due to new immigrants from Europe. On April 11, 1847, seventeen German families landed at Davenport, followed by more than 250 additional Germans that summer. In 1848, 250 Germans came to Davenport, the first of many from Schleswig-Holstein, following the failure of the 1848 Revolution in Germany. These Forty-Eighters were financially stable, politically liberal, and well-educated, proud of their heritage but eager to be good citizens. By 1854, one-third of Davenport's population—now larger than Rock Island's—was German-speaking, with a German newspaper, _Der Demokrat_ (1850), several musical societies, a German Free School (free from the church), a German theater, and a Turner Society where mind, heart, and body were all exercised. These Germans, and a small number of German Jews, and other immigrants from

Courtesy, Augustana College Library, Special Collections.

Scotland, Ireland, England, and Hungary, gave Davenport a more cosmopolitan air than her sister cities, who received far fewer Europeans.

By 1849, immigrants coming upriver to the new Territory of Minnesota and the Dakotas, and heading west to the Gold Rush in California had turned Rock Island and Davenport into major steamboat ports. In 1845, fewer than forty steamboats traveled the Upper Mississippi. By 1854, boats of some 250-300 tons were making regular stops. In 1854, Rock Island averaged 175 arrivals a month during the season, while arrivals and departures from Davenport had reached 1,587 by 1857. Rock Island, with access to Rock River Valley coal, became the major refueling station above St. Louis, while Davenport became an important supply station for the westward bound as well as a wholesaling center for the hundreds of towns founded by those new settlers.

As steamboat traffic increased, the Rock Island Rapids became more of an obstacle than ever. In 1837, the Chief of Engineers had sent a West Point graduate, Lieutenant Robert E. Lee (later the Con-federate General) to map the rapids and devise improvement methods. Lee and his party lived on the second deck of a steamboat sunk in the rapids, from which, Lee reported, they could fish out the win-

Courtesy, Davenport Public Library.

dows. Appropriations dried up the next year, and Lee did not return. Similar attempts in the 1850s met with little success.

Immigrant traffic created a boom at the head of the rapids. A growing LeClaire absorbed Parkhurst in 1855, and became the headquarters of some 40 or 50 rapids pilots who made their living taking boats up and down 14.7 miles of the Mississippi. As many as 50 other LeClaire residents were captains, pilots, clerks, or engineers. In the off season, LeClaire's population of 700 swelled by another 300 to 400 rivermen who wintered there, attending lyceums and church box suppers, listening to newspapers and good books being read—or occasionally just being rowdy.

Before the Panic of 1857 ended LeClaire's dreams, the town had 18 drygoods stores, a bank, four hotels, five churches, a plow factory, a sawmill and two flour mills, as well as a lyceum and debating society.

The Chicago and Rock Island Rail Road

At 5 p.m. on Washington's Birthday in 1854, a decorated locomotive pulled six bright yellow coaches into the Chicago and Rock Island Rail Road passenger house in Rock Island. Railroad builder Henry Farnham bragged to a large flag-waving crowd that Rock Island was now only 42 hours from New York. The year before, a trip to Chicago alone took two weeks by wagon.

The railroad had been nine years in the making. Two weeks before his death, Colonel Davenport hosted a meeting of local investors, including Antoine LeClaire and Judge James Grant of Daven-port, to plan a railroad east from Rock Island to LaSalle, the terminus of the Illinois and Michgan Canal. Local interest in railroads was part of a national railroad fever brought on by sectional competition for an east-west rail route. Southerners were pushing for a route through New Orleans to San Diego, Northerners for a route through Chicago to San Francisco. The Tri-Cities not only lay in the most direct line of the Chicago route, but the narrow channel, the island, and the solid bedrock on both shores made this a likely crossing point.

There were no plans to stop the line at Rock Island. An Iowa company was already laying tracks west across Iowa. Construction of a rail road bridge began in 1854, even before the tracks reached Rock Island.

Henry Farnham held a grand opening for the Chicago and Rock Island Rail Road in June of 1854. On June 5, more than 1,200 guests, including Millard Fillmore, 13th President of the United States, Charles Dana, editor of the *New York Tribune*, and the historian George Bancroft, arrived at Rock Island from Chicago in two trains. They boarded five waiting steamboats for a gala trip to Fort Snelling and the Falls of St. Anthony, a publicity gimmick which made the railroad famous, a fame it kept well into the 20th century as the Rock Island Lines.

On April 22, 1856, the Rock Island Bridge opened to traffic and to the dismay of steamboaters. The bridge was located at a point in the rapids which many felt was deliberately chosen to interfere with navigation. The drawspan sat at an angle to the current. Both sides realized that this was more than a local fight. Two major Midwestern commercial centers were competing for the title of Queen City, the river port of St. Louis and an upstart Chicago with the railroad as its weapon.

On May 6, 1856, the Rock Island Bridge became a battlefield in that war. As the steamer *Effie Afton* passed the drawspan, one of her paddles stopped, and the current carried her back against the bridge. Nearby boats rescued the crew and passengers, but the boat caught fire, damaged the bridge, and sank.

In a test case closely watched in Chicago and St. Louis, and by other railroads planning to bridge the Mississippi, the owners of the *Effie Afton* sued the bridge company for damages. The case came before the Federal court in Chicago, where Abraham Lincoln served as one of the lawyers for the M & M Bridge Company. A subsequent suit between bridge and steamboat interests eventually reached the Supreme Court, which, in 1872, decided for the bridge, a ruling that precipitated bridge construction up and down the Mississippi. The Rock Island Bridge continued to menace navigation until a new bridge downstream replaced it in 1872. Of the 1,677 boats passing the bridge in 1857, 50 collided with the structure.

The Tri-Cities on the Eve of the Civil War

Competition between steamboat and railroad lowered rates by opening a more direct route to the East. A greater choice in shipping brought the Tri-Cities new manufacturing concerns which laid the foundations for today's much larger industries. In Moline, the Dimock & Gould Woodenware Company with its automated assembly line, and the Deere factory, making more than 400 plows a week and shipping to England, were joined in 1854 by the Moline Iron Works of Williams, Heald & Company (later Williams, White) and the Moline Wagon Company. In 1855, the Buford & Tate Plow Company opened in Rock Island, and in 1856, the Davenport Iron Works opened with fifty-five employees. By 1860, the Tri-Cities had thirty manufacturing concerns, not counting the many small custom shops.

As Davenport, Rock Island, and Moline grew from river towns to mercantile and industrial centers, their appearance and their culture changed. Rock Island and Davenport were platted on less than 100 acres; by 1856, Davenport had grown to 2,000 acres with a population of more than 10,000, and Rock Island had grown to 1,500 acres with more than 5,000 people. Between August 1, l856, and the end of 1857, 1,300 houses were built in Davenport alone. Downtowns grew up.

By 1856, Davenport and Rock Island both had new gas streetlights. "Now 400 train passengers won't have to grope their way to hotels," the *Rock Island Argus* bragged. Many individual stores were replaced during the 1850s by large three and four story buildings called "blocks," housing several businesses. In Rock Island the Bailey and Boyle Block and the Buford Block citified the downtown, as did businesses like the New York Store in Moline. Davenport's new

JOHN M. GOULD WAS PRESIDENT AND MANAGING DIRECTOR OF THE DIMOCK AND GOULD WOODENWARE COMPANY. THIS PARTNERSHIP MANUFACTURED SMALL WOODENWARE. BY 1858, THE BUSINESS CHANGED TO DIMOCK, GOULD AND COMPANY AND A SAWMILL AND LUMBER YARD WERE ADDED.

Courtesy, Rock Island County Historical Society.

During the 1850s, many stores moved into "blocks," which were large three and four story buildings. These "blocks" housed several businesses and were situated all over the Tri-Cities. This view shows the Mitchell and Lynde Block in downtown Rock Island.

blocks, Metropolitan Hall, Nickoll's Block, Cook & Sargent's Bank, and others designed by professional architects, together with the LeClaire Block and the new railroad hotel, the Burtis House (five stories, hot and cold water, and gas lights) made an Eastern gentlemen confess that "you can hardly think it possible that you are more than 1,000 miles from Philadelphia."

The appearance of larger building units was paralleled by a broadening of cultural life. By 1856, Davenport alone had five daily newspapers and several weeklies. Lyceums began inviting outside talent to the Tri-Cities. Horace Greeley, Artemus Ward, Ralph Waldo Emerson, and Ole Bull performed here.

Theater expanded from minstrel shows and melodramas to Shakespeare in LeClaire Hall, a "real theater." The Davenport Philharmonic Society organized in 1856, performed Handel's *Messiah* twice in 1857-58.

The Tri-Cities had always been proud of the education they could offer—the *Davenport Gazette* bragged in 1850 of having ten schools in a town of 1,400, so that a student "might commence with letters, and without leaving town, graduate in all the higher branches of an English education, with a knowledge of the dead languages and very many of the living ones"—but by the mid-1850's, all three towns had outgrown the often transient private schools meeting in homes. Davenport built its first

Mount Ida Ladies College was founded in 1855 in Davenport by Thales Lindsay as an institute to train women to teach. It was located on the bluff near present day College and Bridge Avenues. During the Civil War, the school building was taken by Camp McClellan soldiers for living quarters, and after the war it never reopened.

Iowa College opened in Davenport in 1848. It was the first place in the Tri-Cities where one could achieve an education beyond high school. When Iowa College moved to Grinnell, Iowa, in 1859, Griswold College was established on its campus.

Courtesy, Putnam Museum.

public school in 1850, and in 1858 became the first town in Iowa to establish a citywide school district under a single superintendant and board. Moline built its first public school in 1853, and in 1856, Rock Island became one of the first schools in Illinois to consolidate its three public schools into a single district.

Education beyond high school was available as early as 1848 when a non-sectarian school, Iowa College, opened in Davenport. In 1849, a new College of Physicians and Surgeons moved from Rock Island to Davenport, and trained 36 doctors before moving to Keokuk and eventually becoming the medical school of the University of Iowa. Thales Lindsay established his Ladies College in Davenport in 1855 to train women to teach. It was Lindsay who proposed that the United States establish a national university on the island, and outlined a sixteen year program of

"laborious study." When Iowa College moved to Grinnell, Iowa, in 1859, Episcopalians established Griswold College on its campus.

Interest in education also led to the beginnings of libraries and literary societies. In 1855, T. J. Buford and others organized the Rock Island City Library and Reading Room Association in the Bailey and Boyle Block with a librarian and 1,000 books. By 1856 Jewish immigrants organized a Young Men's Hebrew Literary Association for young men from Rock Island and Davenport. In Davenport, the banker George B. Sargent donated $500 to the Carey Reading Room to open a collection of books to the public, and Moline followed with a similar organization in 1857.

By 1860, the Tri-Cities had developed distinct personalities still in evidence today in both their

Charles Atkinson was one of the founders of Moline. The surveyor of the original plat drew up two maps, on one of which he had written "Moline" and the other, "Hesperia." When the surveyor explained to the founders that Moline stood for mills, and Hesperia meant "Star of the West," Atkinson is said to have remarked, "Moline let it be."

Courtesy, Rock Island County Historical Society.

Courtesy, Rock Island County Historical Society.

Charles Deere, son of John Deere, became the owner of the Deere Company at the age of twenty-one. John Deere had been forced to transfer ownership to his son in order to avoid bankruptcy. Charles Deere ran the company for the next forty-nine years.

attitudes and their architecture. Davenport had become a busy, diversified commercial center, less dependent on the river than it had been. Its varied ethnic groups made it seem cosmopolitan. Rock Island was still tied closely to the river, its activities centering on the levee. To many visitors, it felt "southern," a result of its immigrants from the upland south, the most prominent of which were the Bufords. Two of John Buford's sons served as mayors of Rock Island; Napoleon Buford enlarged his father's store into a pork packing plant, and went on to become a banker and president of a railroad. An uncle, Charles Buford, provided the capitol for the Buford and Tate Plow Works, and built a large Gothic Revival mansion on 7th Avenue.

East of Rock Island lay the no-nonsense manufacturing town of Moline. The surveyor of the original plat drew up two maps, on one of which he had written "Moline" and the other, "Hesperia." When he explained to the founders that Moline stood for mills, and Hesperia meant "Star of the West," Charles Atkinson is said to have remarked, "Moline let it be." Moline's leaders, John Deere, Charles Atkinson, the Dimocks and the Goulds, passed their New England work ethic on to their employees. Deere warned one of those employees that his neighbors would never amount to much "because they ate two spreads on their bread." If the work ethic produced a staid atmosphere—"a much duller town could not be scared up this side of Sleepy Hollow," complained an editor of the *Moline Workman* in 1854—it was also dependable. "In Moline," wrote one resident in 1857, "very little is left to chance or the devil."

The Panic of 1857 ended boom times. The Tri-Cities survived better than LeClaire and other small villages, but all three cities lost population and were left with tenantless houses as hundreds of residents left to look for work. Burrows and Prettyman went bankrupt in 1858, the banking firm of Cook and Sargent a year later. John Deere came close to bankruptcy, saved only by transferring ownership of the firm to his 21 year-old son Charles Deere, who was to run the company for the next 49 years. By 1860, the possibility of war had turned to probability, an event few Tri-Citians welcomed, but all felt powerless to stop.

CHAPTER THREE:

Reshaping the Vision 1860-1900

The Civil War

DURING THE LAST HALF OF THE 1850S, THE OPTIMISM OF TRI-CITIANS WAS OVERSHADOWED BY THE SLAVERY QUESTION. THE KANSAS-Nebraska Act in 1854, permitting new territories to decide whether they would be slave or free, the Dred Scott Decision of 1857 in which the Supreme Court ruled that a slave had no right to sue in Federal court, and the execution of John Brown on December 2, 1859, provoked strong reactions among local citizens. The Dred Scott case, in fact, had begun at Fort Armstrong in 1834, when the slave was taken into free Illinois by his owner, Dr. John Emerson, the post surgeon.

THE DRED SCOTT CASE BEGAN AT FORT ARMSTRONG IN 1834, WHEN SCOTT WAS TAKEN INTO FREE ILLINOIS BY HIS OWNER, DR. JOHN EMERSON, THE POST SURGEON. YEARS LATER, SCOTT SUED FOR HIS FREEDOM, ON THE GROUNDS THAT HIS RESIDENCE IN A FREE STATE HAD MADE HIM A FREE MAN. THE SUPREME COURT RULED THAT A SLAVE HAD NO RIGHT TO SUE IN FEDERAL COURT.

Courtesy, Augustana College Library, Special Collections.

Davenport's liberal Germans were ready to fight in "bleeding Kansas," and helped organize a number of local military groups such as the Davenport Rifles (1857), the Davenport City Artillery (1858), and the Davenport City Guards and the Sarsfield Guards (1858). "There is no city in the West," boasted a Davenporter, "that can equal Davenport in her display of military." When John Brown was hung, Davenport Germans lowered the flag to half-mast over Lahrmann's Hall, and draped their closed stores in mourning. Reverend Hitchcock of the First Congregational Church in Moline kept the abolitionist fires of his flock alive by reminding them that "slavery is a

compromise with hell."

Not so in Rock Island, where many of the original settlers retained their sympathy for the South, if not for slavery. In 1855, J. B. Danforth, editor of the *Rock Island Republican*, changed its name to the *Argus* in response to the new anti-slavery Republican Party.

In the 1860 election, Davenport and Moline voted for Lincoln (4 to 1 in Moline), but in Rock Island, even the parades of the Lincoln Wide Awakes could not keep Lincoln from losing to the pro-slavery parties headed by Douglas, Breckenridge, and Bell.

The *Argus* complained about Lincoln and his "black Republicans;" but when the news of Fort Sumter reached the Tri-Cities on April 13, 1861, even the *Argus* called on its readers to support the Union. All three cities responded quickly to Lincoln's call for

BAILEY DAVENPORT, THE SON OF COLONEL GEORGE DAVENPORT, WAS A SHREWD BUSINESSMAN WHO MADE A FORTUNE IN REAL ESTATE. HE ALSO SERVED AS THE DEMOCRATIC MAYOR OF ROCK ISLAND DURING THE CIVIL WAR.

Courtesy, Augustana College Library, Special Collections.

75,000 three-month volunteers.

By April 16, Davenport Germans had raised a company under August Wentz, which went to St. Louis (with uniforms made by the women of Davenport) to become part of the First Iowa Regiment. The first Rock Island company under Captain W. D. Williams left for Springfield on April 26 amid speeches by Mayor Bailey Davenport and a flag made from the bunting of an earlier Stephen A. Douglas rally. The Rock Island men became Company D of the 12th Illinois Infantry. They fought in the Battle of Shiloh, reinlisted in 1864 in the Army of Tennessee, fought in the Battle and Siege of Atlanta, at Kennesaw Mountain, and on November 11, 1864, they joined Sherman in his march to the sea. When they were discharged on July 18, 1865, the 1,000 men of the 12th Illinois Infantry had been reduced to fewer than 200.

Courtesy, Rock Island Arsenal Museum.

That same April, Robert H. Graham, editor of the *Moline Independent*, raised a cavalry troop and was subsequently captured at the Battle of Lexington and exchanged for Confederate prisoners. Graham then raised two infantry companies, H and I, from Rock Island, Mercer, Henry, and Whiteside counties, and joined the famous 8th Kansas Infantry in the Battles of Atlanta, Nashville, and Missionary Ridge.

Because of its location on the Mississippi, and because the telegraph only came that far, Davenport became the major collecting point for Iowa troops and the emergency location of the state government. The largest of the five collection camps to locate in Davenport was Camp McClellan, established on August 8, 1861, east of the city limits. In 1862, a small section of the camp was partitioned off to hold Indian prisoners of the Sioux Uprising in western Minnesota whom Lincoln had saved from hanging.

Even as citizens of Scott and Rock Island Counties were going to war, the war came to them. The destruction of Harper's Ferry by Confederate troops in 1861 convinced Congress to locate a new arsenal on the island of Rock Island. The site selected lay along the north shore just east of the ruins of Fort Armstrong. Work began on Storehouse A, as the building was called, in 1863.

By July, a second military installation was under construction on the island, a prison to house up to 13,000 Confederate soldiers. By December 1863, nearly 5,600 prisoners—many from the Battle of Lookout Mountain—were living in this city within a city in barracks of 120 men each. Each barracks was allowed to determine its own laws and social life, with the result that gambling dens flourished alongside an

Courtesy, Rock Island Arsenal Museum.

extensive library and courses in French and geography.

Although Margaret Mitchell in *Gone with the Wind* called this prison "the Andersonville of the North," it was neither so large nor so notorious. The mortality rate was below average for Civil War prisons—193.2 per thousand per year compared to Andersonville's 732.6. Still, war wounds, small pox and other diseases, and one of the worst winters on record in 1863-64 resulted in the deaths of 1,964 of the 12,000 prisoners. The prisoners were buried in separate graves in a Confederate cemetery which is still decorated with Confederate flags each Memorial Day.

By the end of the war in April 1865, several Tri-Citians had become heroes. On November 9, 1861, Lieutenant Colonel August Wentz was killed at Belmont. His body was returned to Davenport where he lay in state in Metropolitan Hall. His funeral on November 13 was accompanied by a grand military display while schools and many businesses closed.

Courtesy, Rock Island Arsenal Museum.

General Napoleon Buford (who had suggested to President Lincoln that freed slaves be given their own country in Africa) distinguished himself at the Battle of Belmont. His brother, General John Buford, is today remembered by a statue and plaque at the entrance to the battlefield at Gettysburg as the officer who selected that site for the battle.

As heroic was a Keokuk nurse, Annie Wittenmyer. Ministering to dying soldiers after the surrender of Vicksburg in 1863, and hearing their concerns for their families, she used her position as Iowa State Sanitary Agent to convince Governor Kirkwood to establish homes for children orphaned by the war. In 1865, one of these homes was established on the grounds of Camp Kinsman in Davenport, where Annie Wittenmyer served for two years as matron. The Annie Wittenmyer Home has been in use ever since by several social service agencies.

Revisions

If the Civil War disrupted the lives of Tri-Citians, it did help the local economy recover from the Panic of 1857. In 1863, a group of Davenporters obtained the first certificate issued under the new uniform Federal bank laws, and opened the first national bank in the United States. That same year, the former Mitchell and Lynde Bank of Rock Island became the First National Bank of Rock Island.

Nevertheless, the Tri-Cities at the end of the war were neither models of eastern mill towns such as Lowell, Massachussets, nor full-fledged port cities such as Cincinnati. There were no paved streets, no sewer or water systems, and therefore not a single house with indoor bathrooms. So many cows roamed the streets of Davenport that Washington and Lafayette Squares had to be fenced in. Most important, the steamboat traffic on which the Tri-Cities had depended for much of their growth failed to

Courtesy, Putnam Museum.

The first two-level railroad and wagon bridge between Davenport and Arsenal Island opened in 1872. However, as time passed, heavier and larger locomotives needed a stronger bridge. Remodeling of the bridge began in 1896 and within a year the all-iron bridge was completed.

rebound after the war.

None of this prevented civic leaders from dreaming. A new urban ideal had replaced the Jeffersonian vision of a United States filled with farms and small towns. A Corps of Engineers survey of the Rock River in 1866 resurrected plans for a channel all the way to Lake Michigan and predicted the rise of "Birminghams, Pittsburghs along the Rock River."

For the rest of the century, the model of Pittsburgh rather than Lowell impelled the Tri-Cities to make their downtowns into urban centers. Rock Island changed its streets and avenues to numbers in 1876, after several councilmen visited Philadelphia for the Centennial. Moline followed suit in 1883.

General Thomas J. Rodman took command of the Rock Island Arsenal in 1865. It was Rodman's vision to enlarge the Arsenal to occupy nearly the entire island. Rodman died in 1871 and was buried in the National Cemetery he established on the island.

This vision was aided after the war by the Ordnance Department and the Corps of Engineers. In the summer of 1865, the Ordnance Department sent General Thomas Rodman to take command of the Rock Island Arsenal. He completed Storehouse A, the building begun in 1863, but convinced his superiors to authorize a much larger, national arsenal, occupying nearly the whole island.

Although Secretary of War Jefferson Davis had succeeded in preventing the island from being sold to the public in 1854, the island was home to several sawmills, a chair factory, warehouses, stables, lumberyards, and houses. David Sears had expanded his island operations by buying Benham's Island at the head of Arsenal Island (as the big island now came to be called). Sears had platted a town called Rock Island Village, with a steamboat landing, warehouses, a flour mill, and a road to Moline. These all had to be moved off.

The railroad bridge, too, lay in the way of the new shops, and Rodman replaced it with a two-level railroad and wagon bridge between Davenport and the tip of Arsenal Island near Storehouse A. The Government Bridge was opened to traffic on November 21, 1872, and proved an immediate success in bringing the communities across the river from each other closer together. In 1874, 330,000 foot passengers crossed the bridge.

Work on the expanded arsenal began in the late 1860s. In 1871, General Rodman began work on his

Courtesy, Rock Island Arsenal Museum.

Courtesy, Augustana College Library, Special Collections.

masterpiece, a residence for the arsenal commandant. Quarters One, as the building came to be called, was an impressive Italian Villa-style home, with 19,000 square feet and more than fifty rooms–today the largest Government-owned residence outside the White House. General Rodman died in 1871 before Quarters One was finished, and was buried in the National Cemetery he established on the island. Work on his masterplan was carried out over the next three decades, helping the Tri-Cities weather periodic business depressions better than many similar communities.

In 1866, the Corps of Engineers turned its attention to improving navigation on the Upper Mississippi River. The Government was determined to restore river traffic suspended by the Civil War. On June 23, 1866, Congress appropriated $100,000 for work at the Rock Island Rapids, marking the beginning of a permanent Rock Island District Corps of Engineers.

The Rock Island Rapids consisted of a 14.7-mile stretch of river between Arsenal Island and LeClaire where pools of water separated by fingers of rock extending from both shores created a twisting channel of cross currents and shallows always dangerous and often impossible to navigate. Work on the intractable Rock Island Rapids provided both skilled and unskilled workers with good jobs for the next 75 years.

Before he died, General Rodman resolved a conflict with Moline over the use of waterpower from Sylvan Slough. In 1865, the factories along the Moline waterfront had organized as the Moline Water Power Company under Charles Atkinson to protect their interests. Moline and Rodman worked out an agreement whereby the company deeded all its Sylvan Slough rights to the Government in return for one-fourth of all the power generated. The Government further agreed to construct a power dam across the slough and a 2,400-foot lateral power dam along the Moline waterfront. Construction of the "Great Wall of Moline" began in 1868, and was modified a year later by a 2,100-foot tail race below the dam, cutting off a bulge of land, which became Sylvan Island. Completed in 1872, the lateral dam contained

Courtesy, Rock Island County Historical Society.

Courtesy, Rock Island County Historical Society.

Courtesy, Rock Island Arsenal Museum.

56 sluice gates, each a source for waterpower–power Moline did not outgrow until 1899.

The Moline arrangements forced David B. Sears, the original developer of Sylvan Slough, to new ventures. In 1867, he obtained a charter from Illinois to build dams across all four channels of the Rock River near Vandruff's Island, with a navigation canal at the main channel. Sears' Rock River Navigation and Water Power Company led to a flurry of renewed activity on and near Vandruff's Island. In 1869, Sears platted a community known as Searstown on the north shore of the river near a supply of good clay for a brick factory and pottery. On the island itself, the Rock River Paper Company joined two existing paper mills turning out several tons of wrapping paper a week. In 1873, Sears opened a cotton factory employing 75 to 100 workers who made white and brown duck cloth, flannel, grain and flour sacks, as well as twine, rope and carpet warp. This second attempt at making Vandruff's Island a manufacturing center lasted less than twenty years, as steam power replaced waterpower and as mass production quickly made small local paper and cloth mills obsolete. Searstown was incorporated in 1884 before declining gradually until it was annexed by Rock Island in 1915.

Heavy industries fared much better. Fed by a rapid increase in the mechanization of American farms after the war the use of machinery doubled between 1860 and 1870–farm equipment factories came into their own. In 1860, two plow works in the Tri-Cities, with 70 employees, turned out 18,000 plows a year. By 1870, three companies employing

Courtesy, Rock Island County Historical Society.

Courtesy, Putnam Museum.

Courtesy, Putnam Museum.

511 men turned out 63,000 plows. Deere, incorporated as Deere and Company in 1868, opened its first branch house in Kansas City, Missouri, in 1869, and by 1884 had 12 branch houses from New York to California. Deere and Mansur, the third corn planter factory in the nation, opened in 1877. By 1892, Deere and Company was employing more than 1,000 work-ers in the Tri-Cities alone. Other farm equipment concerns also expanded after the war. Candee, Swan and Company became Moline Plow Company in 1870. The Buford and Tate Company became the Rock Island Plow Works in 1884, making over fifty differ-ent styles of plows. Morris Rosenfield turned a small pre-war factory into the Moline Wagon Company in 1871, the largest wagon-making firm in the country.

Several related industries grew along with the farm equipment businesses. The machine shop of Williams, White and Company was joined by the Moline Malleable Iron Company (1869), the Bettendorf Wheel Works (1890), the Mutual Wheel Company of Moline (1891), and Frank Foundries in Davenport (1898). In 1894, the Deere family opened the Sylvan Steel Mills, a rolling and forging operation producing steel rails, on the island created by the tail race below the Moline power wall.

Rail traffic in and out of the Tri-Cities continued to grow. By 1887, the year the Chicago, Rock Island and Pacific Railroad inaugurated its new Chicago-Kansas City limited, the *G-Whizz*, 72 passenger trains were arriving and departing the Tri-Cities each day on

THE MEAD, SMITH, AND MARSH SAWMILL IN ROCK ISLAND IS SHOWN HERE IN 1857. THIS SAME YEAR, FREDERICK WEYERHAEUSER WAS PUT IN CHARGE OF A BRANCH OF MEAD, SMITH, AND MARSH'S SAWMILL IN COAL VALLEY. WITHIN THREE YEARS, WEYERHAEUSER AND HIS BROTHER-IN-LAW, F.C.A. DENKMANN, OWNED THE COMPANY.

Courtesy, Augustana College Library, Special Collections.

several major and many branch lines. An average of 300 freight cars a day were loaded at Rock Island alone. On the river, meanwhile, steamboat traffic had all but ended. Fewer than 1,000 passengers boarded boats at Davenport in 1887, most of them for short excursions.

The growing need for coal for trains and factories led to a rapid increase in Rock River Valley coal production. The 60,000 tons mined in 1860 grew to 263,000 tons coming out of 46 mines by 1873.

Smaller Tri-Cities industries also benefitted from the post-war economy. Between 1860 and 1890, the number of manufacturing concerns increased

four-fold, and included furniture factories, breweries, a glass works, the manufacture of stoves and saws, and thirty separate cigar factories in Davenport. By 1885, Rock Island had 435 business and professional establishments, while Davenport had more than 700.

Sawmilling

The most dramatic story of the Tri-Cities after the war was sawmilling. From 1865 until 1895, sawmills dominated both the landscape and the economies of most area communities. Early mills were small, using timber from adjacent bluffs, and serving the needs of local communities. These operations might have increased naturally after the

FREDERICK WEYERHAEUSER WAS BORN IN 1834 IN GERMANY AND CAME TO THE UNITED STATES IN 1852. WEYERHAEUSER CAME TO ROCK ISLAND IN 1856 AND MARRIED F.C.A. DENKMANN'S SISTER-IN-LAW THE FOLLOWING YEAR. WEYERHAEUSER AND DENKMANN BECAME PARTNERS IN 1860 WHEN THEY BOUGHT THE ROCK ISLAND SAWMILL.

Courtesy, Quad City Times.

Courtesy, Augustana College Library, Special Collections.

FREDERICK CARL AUGUST (F.C.A.) DENKMANN WAS BORN IN 1821 IN PRUSSIA AND CAME TO THE UNITED STATES IN 1849. DENKMANN'S EVENTUAL PARTNERSHIP WITH FREDERICK WEYERHAEUSER HELPED TO MAKE THE TRI-CITIES ONE OF THE LARGEST LUMBER MILLING CENTERS ON THE UPPER MISSISSIPPI.

Courtesy, Augustana College Library, Special Collections.

Courtesy, Putnam Museum.

war as logs began coming down the Mississippi from Wisconsin, and the railroad made the Tri-Cities an ideal lumber shipping point, but it would not likely have become a great industry had it not been for a German immigrant, Frederick Weyerhaeuser. Weyerhaeuser came to Rock Island in 1856 to lay rail road track. In 1857, the Mead, Smith, and Marsh sawmill in Rock Island put him in charge of a branch in Coal Valley. Three years later, he and his brother-in-law, F. C. A. Denkmann, owned the company.

Weyerhaeuser and Denkmann were a match. Denkmann supervised the mill doubling its output in a year. Weyerhaeuser was the salesman and entrepreneur. In 1869, in order to fill a large contract for lumber, Weyerhaeuser bought several stands of white pine along the Chippewa River in Wisconsin.

Other sawmills were logging the same area, causing huge jams at the mouth of the Chippewa and confusion over which company owned which logs. To coordinate these chaotic operations, Weyerhaeuser in

1871 organized seventeen Upper Mississippi mills, including the mills of Dimock and Gould, and Keator and Wilson in Moline, and the Schricker and Mueller Mill in Davenport, into the Mississippi River Logging Company. The company bought land together in Wisconsin and built a large holding pen, the Beef Slough Boom, at the mouth of the Chippewa where logs were tied into rafts as large as 300 feet by 1,500 feet, covering eight acres. At first, these rafts were simply floated down the river by a crew of fifteen to twenty men living on board, but in 1869, the Van Sant Company in LeClaire designed a steamboat specifically to push the rafts downriver. The first such boat, the *J. W. Van Sant*, took a Weyerhaeuser and Denkmann raft down to Rock Island in 1870.

Mechanized rafting allowed company mills to increase production far beyond previous levels. During the rafting season, as many as 1,550 men worked at the Beef Slough Boom assembling company rafts. Log rafts were by far the dominant traffic on the Mississippi after the Civil War. A record 1,056

RIGHT *The great fire of 1901 in East Davenport destroyed many homes and businesses, including the Weyerhaeuser and Denkmann sawmill in Davenport. This was just one sign of the downfall of the lumber industry in the Tri-Cities.*

BELOW LEFT *The first horse-drawn streetcar crossed the new tracks from South Rock Island to Milan in 1903. It had taken a while for this mode of transportation to reach Milan. A horse-drawn streecar began operations betwen Moline and Rock Island thirty-five years earlier.*

BELOW RIGHT *Inter-urban rail cars such as this one were a common form of transportation to many areas inside and outside the Tri-Cities. Inter-urban rail car number 404 is shown here with a carload of passengers on the Davenport, Muscatine, Moline and Rock Island system.*

Courtesy, Rock Island Arsenal Museum.

Courtesy, Rock Island County Historical Society.

Courtesy, Putnam Museum.

LEFT *The Moline and Rock Island Horse Railway Company began streetcar operations in 1868. Each 14-passenger horse-drawn car could make the round trip between Moline and Rock Island in half a day. Davenport followed the next year with the Davenport Central Railway Company.*

Courtesy, Putnam Museum.

THE BURTIS HOTEL WAS BUILT ADJACENT TO THE BURTIS OPERA HOUSE, SEEN ON THE LEFT, IN 1873. THE HOTEL NAME WAS CHANGED TO THE KIMBALL HOUSE IN 1880. WITHIN THIRTY YEARS, THE HOTEL BECAME AN APARTMENT BUILDING AND ITS FINAL NAME, THE VALE APARTMENTS, WAS ITS LAST. THE HOTEL WAS RAZED IN DECEMBER OF 1992.

Courtesy, Rock Island Arsenal Musuem.

rafts passed the Government Bridge in 1884.

The astuteness of Weyerhaeuser and Denkmann together with good waterpower and rail transportation made the Tri-Cities one of the largest milling centers on the Upper Mississippi. Between 1858 and 1898, local mills supplied 40% of the total lumber sawed by the seven major mill centers along the river. During the peak year of 1890, Tri-Cities mills employed 2,000 men and sawed 213,629,000 board feet of lumber.

By 1890, it was clear that the white pine forests were giving out. In 1892 Weyerhaeuser moved to St. Paul to be closer to operations that were already moving west. The Weyerhaeuser and Denkmann mill in Rock Island shut down at 8 p.m., November 18, 1905, as the last log climbed from the river to the mill. In the summer of 1915, the *Otumwa Belle* took the last raft of Minnesota white pine down the river. Charles Russell, a longtime raftsman, reflected that "In the literature of waste, this is our *Iliad*."

Downtowns

Meanwhile, the Tri-Cities rapidly grew into small copies of their Eastern counterparts. On October 29, 1868, the Moline and Rock Island Horse Railway Company began streetcar operations between Moline and Rock Island, each 14-passenger horse drawn car making the round trip in half a day. The Davenport Central Railway Company began operations the following March. A steam-powered car had replaced horses (which wore out too fast) on Brady Street hill by 1878. In 1885, Moline became the first city in Illinois (and only the third in the United

States) to have electric street cars, followed by Davenport in 1888, and Rock Island a year later. In 1889, all three cities' car lines were consolidated as the Tri-City Railway Company.

City waterworks in Rock Island (1871) and Davenport (1873) led to modern hotels and stores. In 1869, after his hotel, the Rodman House, burned, Ben Harper, one-time mayor of Rock Island, determined to build the finest hotel on the rail line between Chicago and the West Coast "to show visitors we have enterprise here and faith in the future." The Harper Opera House, with its 1,200-seat auditorium, opened in 1871, the first hotel in the west to have fire escapes. It joined the Burtis Opera House in Davenport (1867) in hosting international celebrities such as Mark Twain, Sarah Bernhardt, Buffalo Bill, Susan B. Anthony, and Tom Thumb.

Rock Island's reputation as a shopping center grew in 1870 with the opening of L. S. McCabe's Plunder Store selling household goods and personal items in separate areas or "departments" within the store. An innovative advertiser, McCabe offered two sales each year before the August and January sewings, where women could pick out material to be sewn into garments by McCabe seamstresses. In 1874, Rock Island created the Star Block on the east side of Spencer Square complete with water, gas, bathrooms, and "every modern convenience." By the end of the century, Davenport had even larger department stores. Petersen's and Sons Department Store opened in 1892, followed by R. H. Harned and C. J. Von Maur's Boston Store in 1898. By then, Davenport and Rock Island had both begun to pave their streets—

Courtesy, Rock Island County Historical Society.

Courtesy, Bawden Brothers Collection, Putnam Museum.

Courtesy, Putnam Museum.

Rock Island with miles of brick paving.

Modernization attracted the other necessities of urban living. In 1868, in cooperation with Scott County, the Sisters of Mercy opened Mercy Hospital in Davenport. Rock Island's first hospital, 12-bed St. Luke's, opened in the west end in 1884, and was replaced with a much larger St. Anthony's Hospital in 1892. A second Davenport hospital, St. Luke's, opened in 1895 with a training school for nurses. Moline City Hospital opened the following year. In 1896, the State of Illinois began construction of the Western Illinois Hospital for the Insane east of Moline in an unincorporated area known as Watertown. All three cities established public libraries in the 1870s,

Rock Island in 1872, Moline in 1873, and Davenport (Cook Memorial Library) in 1877.

The post Civil War period also brought the first public high school graduates. Davenport graduated its first class of nine in 1871. Rock Island graduated its first class–five girls–in 1874, with ceremonies at the Harper Opera House and an address by F. C. A. Denkmann. The entire class was then hired to teach in the Rock Island system. Five girls and one boy became Moline's first graduates in 1876.

Davenport's liberal bent showed up in its school board, which appointed the first woman superintendent of schools in Iowa (and perhaps in the nation) in 1874. Phebe Sudlow had begun teaching in Davenport

Courtesy, Putnam Museum.

CLASSES BEGAN AT AUGUSTANA COLLEGE AND SEMINARY IN ROCK ISLAND IN THE FALL OF 1875. OLD MAIN, THE DOMED BUILDING SHOWN HERE, WAS NOT COMPLETED UNTIL 1894. THE CAMPUS WAS ESTABLISHED NEAR THE CENTER OF SWEDISH-LUTHERAN IMMIGRATION.

Courtesy, Rock Island County Historical Society.

Courtesy, Rock Island County Historical Society.

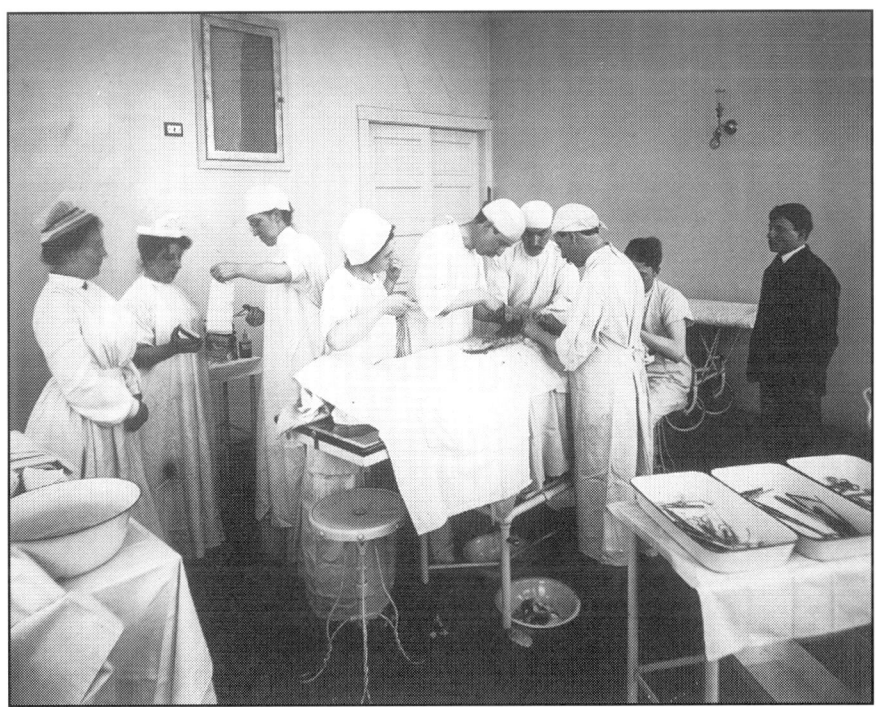

Courtesy, Putnam Museum.

ABOVE LEFT THE STATE OF ILLINOIS BEGAN CONSTRUCTION OF THE WESTERN ILLINOIS HOSPITAL FOR THE INSANE IN 1896. THE HOSPITAL WAS BUILT EAST OF MOLINE IN AN UNINCORPORATED AREA KNOWN AS WATERTOWN. THIS PHOTO WAS TAKEN AROUND 1900 AND SHOWS "PATIENTS IN THE TURNIP PATCH."

ABOVE RIGHT THE EPISCOPAL DIOCESE OPENED ST. KATHERINE'S HALL AS A PREP SCHOOL FOR GIRLS IN DAVENPORT IN 1884. BOYS WERE ALLOWED TO ATTEND THE SCHOOL THROUGH FIFTH GRADE. THIS VIEW SHOWS THE GRADUATION CLASS OF 1897.

LEFT THE SISTERS OF MERCY OPENED MERCY HOSPITAL IN 1868 IN DAVENPORT. ROCK ISLAND'S FIRST HOSPITAL, 12-BED ST. LUKE'S, OPENED IN 1884, AND WAS REPLACED WITH A MUCH LARGER ST. ANTHONY'S HOSPITAL IN 1892. THIS PHOTO SHOWS AN OPERATION IN PROGRESS AT MERCY HOSPITAL.

Courtesy, Bawden Brothers Collection, Putnam Museum.

in 1858. She became the high school principal in 1872, before becoming superintendent of schools, a post she accepted only after the board agreed to bring her salary up to what a man would be paid.

Private and parochial high schools continued to prosper. The Episcopal Diocese opened St. Katherine's Hall as a school for girls and boys in 1884. The Villa de Chantal moved here from Maysville, Kentucky, in 1899 to train young women. In 1875, Augustana College and Seminary (with a high school preparatory academy) moved to the east edge of Rock Island in 1875 to be close to a growing center of Swedish Lutheran immigration. The new Davenport Diocese organized St. Ambrose College in 1882.

One of the most distinctive of Tri-Cities institutions began 1895 when D. D. Palmer began making spinal adjustments on his patients. In 1897, he opened a school, the Palmer Institute and Chiropractic Infirmary, which became the Palmer College of Chiropractic in 1905 under his son, B. J. Palmer.

As eastern industrial cities had already discovered, urbanization did not come without a price. As the Tri-Cities modernized and expanded (Rock Island had grown by 72 additions to its original boundaries by 1884), they awoke to new social and economic problems. The poor, homeless, and those out of work drifted into shanty towns along the flood plains or into the older and now-deteriorating sections of town, while the rich went up the hill to build homes (approaching castles along the Davenport bluffs or with understated elegance in Moline), or withdrew into their own enclave (as in Rock Island's Silk Stocking Row, part of the area now being restored as the Broadway Historic District).

European immigrants after the war often found themselves in neighborhoods formed along ethnic or economic lines. In Rock Island, families of Jewish immigrants from eastern Europe, less wealthy and more traditional in their religion than the German Jews who had quickly integrated into business and civic life in the 1850s, created a Jewish neighborhood between Second and Fourth Avenues and Twelfth to Sixteenth Streets in which the Shomre Shaboth congregation kept traditional worship.

Sin, the unwanted immigrant, also staked out its own neighborhoods, especially in Rock Island and Davenport where taverns and gambling dens clustered along the waterfront, attracting raftsmen and transient sawmill laborers as well as locals. In Davenport, an especially notorious area known as Bucktown developed along the river three blocks east of Brady Street. Here flourished a conglomeration of more than 150 saloons, gambling parlors and houses of prostitution with names like Brick Munro's Dance Hall, the Senate Saloon, and Wiggles Theater. Floating dance halls tied up at nearby islands and sloughs, ready to float out across state lines in case of trouble.

Courtesy, Rock Island Arsenal Museum.

Courtesy, Putnam Museum.

Courtesy, Putnam Museum.

LEFT *THE CLARISSA C. COOK HOME FOR THE FRIENDLESS, IN THE WEST END OF DAVENPORT, WAS ESTABLISHED IN 1880 WITH A MAJOR ENDOWMENT FROM COOK'S WILL. THIS HOME WAS MAINLY FOR ELDERLY WOMEN. THIS PHOTO SHOWS SOME OF THE RESIDENTS AND POSSIBLY SOME OF THE EMPLOYEES.*

CENTER LEFT *THE OUTING CLUB WAS OPENED ON BRADY STREET IN DAVENPORT IN 1891 AS A SOCIAL AND RECREATIONAL CENTER. REVEREND ARTHUR M. JUDY, PASTOR OF DAVENPORT'S FIRST UNITARIAN CHURCH, ESTABLISHED THE CLUB AS AN IMITATION OF SIMILAR CLUBS ON THE EAST COAST.*

BELOW LEFT *MODERN WOODMEN OF AMERICA, THE FRATERNAL INSURANCE SOCIETY, WAS FOUNDED IN 1883. THE NEW HOME OFFICE BUILDING WAS CONSTRUCTED IN ROCK ISLAND IN 1898. THE CORNER-STONE DEDICATION WAS HELD ON APRIL 27, 1898, WITH WILLIAM JENNINGS BRYAN AS THE KEYNOTE SPEAKER. THIS VIEW SHOWS THE DEDICATION CEREMONY.*

BELOW RIGHT *THE DAVENPORT ACADEMY OF SCIENCES WAS ORGANIZED IN 1867. IT SOON GREW INTO ITS OWN BUILDING WITH RESEARCH ROOMS AND AN EXTENSIVE LIBRARY. IN 1896, A PATRON, W.C. PUTNAM, WILLED THE ACADEMY SOME REAL ESTATE IN DAVENPORT TO USE PRODUC-TIVELY. TODAY, THE OLD ACADEMY OF SCIENCES HAS BECOME THE PUTNAM MUSEUM.*

Courtesy, Davenport Public Library.

Courtesy, Rock Island County Historical Society.

Courtesy, Putnam Museum.

Several social service organizations appeared, most often women's groups, in response to these social ills. If the city fathers were concerned about the growing social problems, it was more often than not women's groups who set up the network of social service agencies in the Tri-Cities. By the late 1870s, Moline women had organized active chapters of the Women's Christian Temperance Union and a Moline Equal Suffrage Association. In response to increasing numbers of women entering the workforce, the Moline Woman's Club opened a clubroom where women could relax and get a hot meal. The Moline Unitarian Ladies Aid Society, with help from women of other churches, began a free girls cooking school..

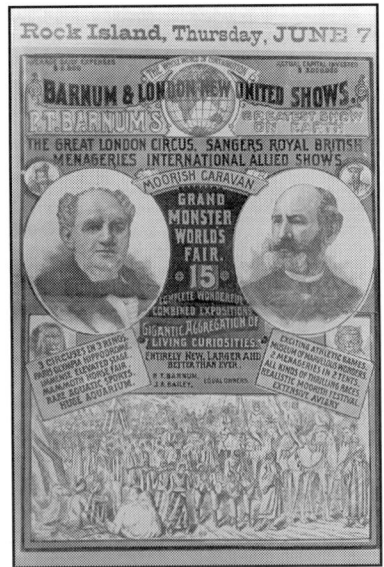

Davenport women were equally active. The Clarissa C. Cook Home for the Friendless opened in 1880, established with money from Cook's will (she had previously helped fund the Davenport Public Library). The King's Daughters opened the Lend-A-Hand Club in 1887 as a place to stay for women coming to the city to work. In 1892, the Ladies Industrial Relief Society opened a center to help women help themselves by learning to sew and cook.

Tri-Cities trade unions also helped make life better for the laborer. Under the leadership of the Knights of Labor, Tri-City unions organized the Rock Island Industrial Home Association in 1887, and in 1894 built a three-story brick building at Third Avenue and Twenty-first Street in Rock Island as a club house, meeting place, gym, and store for laborers.

Two organizations are still active. In 1895, Reverend Edward Lee opened the People's Union Mission in Davenport. In 1911, it was reorganized along the lines of Hull House in Chicago and re-named Friendly House. In 1898, after finding an abandoned infant, Reverend Gottlieb German and his wife opened a kindergarten for Rock Island poor. They incorporated in 1899 as the Union Mission, which in 1902 changed its name to Bethany Home.

For the majority of Tri-Cities citizens, however, urban life in the last half of the 19th century

Courtesy, Rock Island Arsenal Museum.

Philemon Mitchell organized a baseball team known as the Wapellos. At their home field, Bailey Davenport's pasture, they defeated Davenport 118-27 and Peoria 85-24. In 1897, Rock Island joined the Western Association, bringing minor league ball to the Tri-Cities. City parks were supplemented by several private parks. In Davenport, the German Schutzen Verein (shooting club) built a 20-acre park in the west end in 1870, with caves, ravines, and walkways, as well as a shooting gallery, a music stand, and an awards hall. Flambo Gardens up on the bluffs became a favorite Sunday picnic spot. Three amusement parks operated by the streetcar line opened on the Illinois side in the 1890s. Those at Campbell's Island near Watertown, and at Prospect Park in Moline, were modest, but Blackhawk's Watch Tower on the bluff above Saukenuk grew into an extensive amusement park attracting 50,000 people a year, including tourists from outside the area. In addition

SHOOT-THE-CHUTES WAS A HUGE ATTRACTION AT THE AMUSEMENT PARK AT BLACK HAWK'S WATCH TOWER. THIS RIDE SENT BOATLOADS OF CUSTOMERS DOWN A LONG WOODEN SLIDE INTO THE ROCK RIVER. THIS AMUSEMENT PARK ATTRACTED 50,000 PEOPLE A YEAR.

was good. In Davenport, by 1887, there were 55 lodges, 16 secret societies, and 460 other organizations–many of them for women–devoted to entertainment or to improving mind, body, heart, or community standing. Many of these imitated Eastern models. In 1891, the Reverend Arthur M. Judy, pastor of Davenport's First Unitarian Church, transported a piece of his student days at Harvard to the Tri-Cities by establishing the Outing Club on Brady Street as a social and recreational center.

One post-war institution was homegrown. In 1867, four collectors of scientific artifacts organized the Davenport Academy of Sciences, which soon grew into its own building with research rooms and an extensive library. In 1906, the will of a patron, W. C. Putnam, established a real estate trust and instructed it to use his downtown Davenport property to support the Academy. In 1910, the Trust erected an 8-story building on the site, using income from this Putnam Building to maintain the Academy and its museum. Today, the old Academy of Sciences has become the Putnam Museum of History and Natural Science, an important community resource for regional and local history.

Organized sports came to the Tri-Cities in 1866 when a grocer, William Dart, and Rock Island banker

to a grand pavilion, the park offered a shooting gallery, a roller skating rink, a figure-8 roller coaster (the first west of Chicago), and the most popular attraction, a ride known as Shoot-the-chutes which sent boatloads of customers down a long wooden slide into the Rock River.

At the end of the 19th century, Tri-Citians looked back with satisfaction on their progress and forward with anticipation to the new century. Like an Horatio Alger hero, the Tri-Cities had "made something of themselves in this world."

CHAPTER FOUR:

The Age of Industry 1900-1945

New Towns

EAST OF DAVENPORT, IN 1900, IN SIGHT OF THE RISING TRI-CITIES SKYLINE, LAY A BOTTOMLAND ALONG THE MISSISSIPPI LITTLE CHANGED SINCE before the Civil War. An easterner, Elias S. Gilbert, had come here in 1850 to develop a number of farm and small business enterprises. In order to house his

Courtesy, The Children's Museum Foundation.

laborers, Gilbert platted 29 lots along present-day State Street from 10th to 14th Streets. The name became Gilbert on June 30, 1858, though it was never incorporated.

The rich land around Gilbert supported a number of crops, but it was onions which had won out by 1900, thriving in the bottomland soil. By then, Gilbert was a village of German immigrants where "everybody had a picket fence and a garden, and chickens, and a cow and a few pigs."

Then, "overnight," as one historian put it, "the steady people of Gilbert . . . awoke in a whirl of industry, with chimneys that smoke, and wheels that hum, mammoth hydraulic presses that make steel cars and shears that chew up boiler plate." The responsibility for this transformation lay with two brothers, William P. and Joseph Bettendorf, sons of German immigrants. William had invented the first power lift sulky plow and the Bettendorf Metal Wheel. In 1895, he and his brother founded the Bettendorf Axle Company in Davenport. As with the Deeres and the Weyerhaeuser-Denkmann parnership, the brothers complemented each other. William was the inventor while Joseph provided the management genius to run the company.

When a fire in May of 1902 destroyed the Bettendorf factory, Davenport businessmen subscribed $15,000 to buy the remainder of the old Gilbert farm along the tracks of the Davenport, Rock Island, and Northwestern Railroad. The new plant

Courtesy, The Children's Museum Foundation.

ABOVE LEFT *ELIAS S. GILBERT CAME TO THE TRI-CITIES FROM THE EAST IN 1850. HE DEVELOPED A NUMBER OF FARM AND SMALL BUSINESS ENTERPRISES AND BY 1858, THE AREA WAS NAMED GILBERT. THE GILBERT HOME STOOD ON THE PRESENT SITE OF OUR LADY OF LOURDES CHURCH IN BETTENDORF.*

LEFT *MANY DIFFERENT CROPS WERE SUPPORTED ON THE LAND AROUND GILBERT, BUT BY 1900 ONIONS BECAME THE MAIN PRODUCT GROWN IN THE RICH SOIL. ONION GROWING MATURED INTO A LONG AND PROSPEROUS INDUSTRY. YOUNG WORKERS ARE SHOWN HERE HARVESTING A CROP OF ONIONS.*

The Age of Industry **39**

RIGHT *WILLIAM P. AND HIS BROTHER JOSEPH BETTENDORF WERE SONS OF GERMAN IMMIGRANTS. LEFT WILLIAM INVENTED THE FIRST POWER LIFT SULKY PLOW AND THE BETTENDORF METAL WHEEL. IN 1895, HE AND JOSEPH FOUNDED THE BETTENDORF AXEL COMPANY IN DAVENPORT. THE BROTHERS COMPLEMENTED EACH OTHER WELL; WILLIAM WAS THE INVENTOR AND JOSEPH WAS THE BUSINESSMAN.*

Courtesy, Rock Island County Historical Society.

Courtesy, Rock Island County Historical Society.

CENTER RIGHT *THE FOUNDRY ADDITION OF 1909 TO THE BETTENDORF AXEL COMPANY TRIPLED THE PLANT'S SIZE. THE NEW AUTOMATED ASSEMBLY LINE EXTENDED FOR ALMOST A MILE ALONG THE MISSISSIPPI. THE VIEW SHOWS THE FOUNDRY IN THE FOREGROUND AND THE LAVISH JOSEPH BETTENDORF HOME IN THE BACKGROUND. THE HOME IS NOW ST. KATHERINE'S/ST. MARK'S SCHOOL.*

BELOW RIGHT *THE WILLIAM BETTENDORF MANSION WAS COMPLETED IN THE FALL OF 1910. UNFORTUNATELY , WILLIAM DIED IN JUNE OF 1910 AND NEVER LIVED IN THE HOME. TODAY, IT SERVES AS THE IOWA MASONIC NURSING HOME AT 26TH AND STATE STREETS IN BETTENDORF.*

Courtesy, Putnam Museum.

opened late in 1902 with 300 employees. On April 28, 1903, employees and other Gilbert residents voted to incorporate the town as Bettendorf.

That same year, William Bettendorf invented a single piece truck frame for railroad cars, an improvement over earlier trucks (the unit that holds the wheels) which were bolted together and often jarred loose. The invention catapulted the Bettendorf Axle Company into a national manufacturer of railroad cars. The 300 employees in 1903 grew to 3,000 by 1920. Plant size tripled in 1909 with the addition of a foundry in which two open-hearth steel furnaces produced 100 tons of steel castings a day. In the new, automated assembly line that extended for almost a mile along the river, raw materials entered one end and a complete railroad car exited the other.

Across the river, two other new towns grew up around industries. East of Moline lay a large tract of land vacant except for an unincorporated settlement known as Watertown and a railroad stop called Port

Courtesy, The Children's Museum Foundation.

Byron Junction. In the 1890s, a land speculator, Edward H. Guyer, obtained an option on 2,500 acres. Although the first sales in 1895 were disappointing, Guyer and his partners in the East Moline Land Company held on, and by 1900 the Marseilles Company, the Union Malleable Iron Works, and the Root and VanderVoort Engineering Company had located on the land.

LEFT *The Union Malleable Iron Works was located in East Moline. This photo, taken in 1918, shows part of the effect of World War I on local industry with women laborers at the iron works.*

BELOW LEFT *Richard Shippen Silvis and his wife Elizabeth came to the Tri-Cities from Pennsylvania in 1854. In 1902, they sold their farm to the Chicago, Rock Island and Pacific Railroad. This land would be an extensive complex of repair shops and switching yards.*

BELOW RIGHT *The Rock Island Lines opened the world's largest locomotive repair shop in 1904. The complex was originally called Vulcan, but when the settlement was platted in 1905, the name was changed to Silvis to honor the original owners. This photo shows the storekeeper offices in Silvis.*

Courtesy, Rock Island County Historical Society.

Courtesy, Rock Island Historical Society.

Courtesy, Rock Island County Historical Society.

The Village of East Moline was incorporated in December 23, 1902, and compressed into a decade what had taken half a century in the older Tri-Cities. A year after it was incorporated, East Moline had a sewer and water system, cement sidewalks, and streetcar service every fifteen minutes. The town was promoted by the *East Moline Enterprise*, (later the *East Moline Herald*), which extolled the many stores, hotels, doctors and lawyers, and jobs. East Moline was incorporated as a city in 1907. By 1910, the population had reached 2,665, and by 1914, East Moline had annexed Watertown. World War I slowed East Moline's growth, but that has not prevented it from challenging Bettendorf for the position of the "Quad" in Quad Cities.

The birth of East Moline in 1902 coincided with a second development still further east. The Chicago, Rock Island, and Pacific Railroad (now the Rock Island Lines) obtained options on more than 800 acres for an extensive complex of repair shops and switching yards. The land was a originally a farm owned by Richard and Elizabeth Silvis, who had come from Pennsylvania in 1854.

In January 1903, the Rock Island Lines announced that it would build the world's largest locomotive repair shop, along with car repair facilities, a signal communication shop, a store depot, and a hump yard for sorting and assembling freight. At first, the railroad called this complex Vulcan, then New Shops when it opened in February of 1904, but when the settlement was platted in 1905, the name was changed to Silvis to honor the original owners.

Industry

The size and complexity of the Bettendorf Company and the Rock Island Yards at Silvis were typical of a 20th century pattern for most large industrial centers. As machinery grew more complex and expensive, small local or regional companies with little capital were absorbed by larger corporations. In 1880, there were 220 farm equipment manufacturers in the United States with an average of 33 employees; by 1900, 94 were left, but with an average of 238 employ-

WILLIAM BUTTERWORTH, SON-IN-LAW OF CHARLES DEERE, BECAME THE PRESIDENT OF DEERE AND COMPANY AND BROUGHT SIX NON-COMPETING COMPANIES INTO THE DEERE FIRM IN 1911. DEERE BOUGHT THE WATERLOO GASOLINE ENGINE COMPANY IN 1918 AND PUT OUT THE FIRST OF A SERIES OF JOHNNY PUTT-PUTTS THAT BECAME FOLK FIGURES IN THE AMERI-CAN LANDSCAPE.

Courtesy, Rock Island Arsenal Museum.

ees. By the end of the Depression, farm equipment manufacturing in the United States was run by a handful of large corporations, survivors of an eat-or-be-eaten competition.

Deere and others in the Tri-Cities had already begun such growth in the 19th century, but it accelerated in the 20th century. The Rock Island Plow Company was acquired by the Weyerhaeuser interests in 1908, and in 1911 absorbed the Smith Manufacturing Company of Chicago. In 1911, Deere and Company reorganized under a new president, William Butterworth, Charles Deere's son-in-law, and bought six non-competing companies around the country. In 1918, Deere bought the Waterloo (Iowa) Gasoline Engine Company. From this factory emerged the Model D tractor, the first of a series of Johnny Putt-putts that became folk figures in the American landscape. The Moline Plow Company followed suit in 1914 by acquiring four farm equipment factories in other cities. Fifteen years later, Moline Plow was itself merged with three other companies to become an even larger Minneapolis-Moline Power Equipment Company.

Local farm equipment manufacturers were joined in 1924 by a rival, International Harvester, attracted to Rock Island by river transportation and dependable labor. The company opened their Tri-City Works in an old Moline Plow factory, changed the name to the Farmall Works in 1927, and began the annual production of thousands of Big Red tractors.

Other Tri-Cities manufacturers caught growth fever in the first three decades of the 20th century. The Voss Washing Machine Company of Davenport

THE VOSS WASHING MACHINE COMPANY IN DAVENPORT INVENTED A HAND-OPERATED, WOODEN WASHING MACHINE, AND BY 1912 HAD BECOME ONE OF THE FIVE LARGEST WASHING MACHINE COMPA-NIES IN THE UNITED STATES. EMPLOYEES ARE SHOWN HERE CRATING WASHING MACHINES IN 1926.

Courtesy, Putnam Museum.

parlayed a wooden, hand-operated washing machine they had invented into a corporation that, by 1912, had become one of the five largest washing machine companies in the United States. The Standard Table Oil Cloth Company, established in Rock Island in 1901, turned out 50,000 miles of oil cloth a year. In 1909, the old Bettendorf Metal Wheel Company of Davenport expanded into the French and Hecht Company.

The public utilities in Davenport, Rock Island, and Moline (electricity, gas, and streetcar lines) had already consolidated in two companies by the turn of the century, and now followed the corporate pattern, becoming part of a large interstate holding company, United Light and Railways, in 1912. When this conglomerate was broken up in 1942, the local corporation became Iowa-Illinois Gas and Electric.

Courtesy, The Children's Museum Foundation.

Even smaller businesses grew larger. By its 43rd anniversary in 1913, McCabe's Department Store in Rock Island had expanded to 9,700 square feet, with 25 separate departments, a branch post office, a telegraph office, an information bureau, a check stand, and a lunch room, as well as rest and reading rooms. An even more successful local business was the cigar store chain run by the Hickey brothers. Store number one opened in Davenport in 1901. By 1951, Hickey Brothers had become the third largest cigar store chain in the country, with 130 stores in 68 cities.

The Tri-Cities was no exception to the love affair with the automobile which appeared on American roads at the turn of the century. By 1904 East Moline's Root and VanderVoort Engineering became R & V Motors, manufacturers of the Knight Motor Car. Several Moline companies manufactured cars: the Deere-Clark Company in 1906, the Midland (driven to San Francisco and back before 1910), the Dreadnought, manufactured by the Moline Automobile Company (with a self-starter and a presto-lite tank for lights), and the Moline Knight in 1917. In about 1908, Arnold Peterson began manufacturing the Meteor automobile in Bettendorf.

Of all the local manufacturers who tinkered with the automobile, the most successful was Willard Lamb Velie, John Deere's grandson. In 1901, Velie founded the Velie Carriage Company in Moline to manufacture wagons. By 1908, the same year Henry Ford introduced the Model T, Velie had begun

Courtesy, Davenport Public Library.

ABOVE LEFT *ARNOLD PETERSEN BEGAN MANUFACTURING THE METEOR AUTOMOBILE IN BETTENDORF AROUND 1908. THE PRODUCTION OF THIS AUTOMOBILE ONLY LASTED ABOUT FOUR YEARS. THIS VENTURE, ALONG WITH MANY OTHERS, SHOWED THE GREAT INTEREST FOR AUTOMOBILES IN THE TRI-CITIES.*

LEFT *THE HICKEY BROTHERS OPENED THEIR FIRST CIGAR STORE IN DAVENPORT IN 1901. HICKEY BROTHERS BECAME THE THIRD LARGEST CIGAR STORE CHAIN IN THE COUNTRY BY 1951. THE MAN ON THE LEFT IS WILLIAM HICKEY AND THE MAN ON THE RIGHT IS PROBABLY DENNIS HICKEY.*

Courtesy, The Children's Museum Foundation.

RIGHT *BETTENDORF SCHOOL WAS BUILT IN 1908 AT PRESENT DAY 16TH STREET AND MISSISSIPPI BOULEVARD. THE SCHOOL'S NAME WAS CHANGED TO WASHINGTON SCHOOL IN 1927, AND LATER BECAME HOME TO THE BETTENDORF CHILDREN'S MUSEUM. STUDENTS AND TEACHERS ARE SHOWN HERE IN FRONT OF THE SCHOOL.*

Courtesy, Davenport Public Library.

Courtesy, Davenport Public Library.

ABOVE LEFT *THE DAVENPORT LEVEE COMMISSION CREATED LECLAIRE PARK ALONG THE MISSISSIPPI IN 1911. THE MUNICIPAL NATATORIUM WAS PART OF THIS RIVERFRONT PROJECT. THIS VIEW SHOWS A GROUP OF CHILDREN POSING IN THE SWIMMING POOL.*

ABOVE RIGHT *SUBURBAN ISLAND WAS A POPULAR SUMMER RECREATION AREA FOR MANY PEOPLE IN THE TRI-CITIES. THIS GROUP OF SWIMMERS WORE THEIR SUBURBAN ISLAND BEACH (SIB) SWIMSUITS FOR THIS PICTURE IN 1910. THE CITY OF DAVENPORT PURCHASED THE ISLAND IN 1918 AND RENAMED IT CREDIT ISLAND.*

RIGHT *THE ISLAND THAT LIEUTENANT JOHN CAMPBELL AND HIS MEN WERE AMBUSHED AT TODAY BEARS HIS NAME. A MONUMENT WAS DEDICATED TO CAMPBELL AND PLACED ON THE ISLAND. A LARGE GROUP OF PEOPLE ARE SHOWN HERE SITTING NEAR THE MONUMENT ON CAMPBELL'S ISLAND.*

Courtesy, Rock Island County Historical Society.

Courtesy, Davenport Public Library.

Courtesy, Rock Island Historical Society.

the 100th anniversary of Lincoln's birth). In 1911, the Davenport Levee Improvement Commission created LeClaire Park along the river, turning a muddy bank into a gateway with new railroad stations, a ferry service using the Kahlke Boatyard's impressive new *Quinlan*, a natatorium, and a new building for the Lend-A-Hand Club.

Popular entertainment and the arts both found ready audiences. Dozens of theaters appeared, even across the street from each other, to satisfy the appetite for the new movies and vaudeville shows. In 1915, Michael Brotman bought the Dreamland Theater in Rock Island, the first of what became a chain of Brotman theaters in Rock Island and Moline. He was assisted in showing silent films at the Dreamland by three sons: Barney played the piano and sang, Isadore played the violin, with Buster on drums.

Culture, too, benefitted from the prosperity of the early 20th century. The Tri-Cities Symphony was founded in 1916 (and became the Quad-Cities Symphony in 1985). Interest in art brought about the Tri-City Art League in 1910, and the organization of the Davenport Art Gallery in 1925—the first municipal art gallery in Iowa. In Davenport, several writers produced a local literary renaissance that brought them national prominence. The elder stateswoman of this group was Alice French, who wrote under the pen name of Octave Thanet, often locating her stories in Davenport. Among other Davenport writers to achieve fame were Floyd Dell, author of *Mooncalf,* and Susan Glaspell who won a Pulitzer Prize in 1931 for *Allison's House.*

Of all the artists who thrived in the Davenport of this period, the best known today is the cornetist, Leon "Bix" Beiderbecke. He achieved fame with the Jeanette Gold Kettle Band in 1926-27 before joining the Paul Whiteman Band. Those who played jazz with Bix never forgot his music, and helped create an

turning out his first car, "Old Maude." Between 1908 and 1928, the Velie factory turned out more than 75,000 automobiles. Moline's chance to become a car capitol ended, however, with the untimely deaths of both W. L. Velie and his son only months apart in 1929.

The automobile brought a new business to the Tri-Cities: the auto dealer. Rock Island's first dealer, John Dee, began selling the Black Crow, in 1901. By 1913, Rock Island had eleven automobile dealers and garages.

Industrial growth brought prosperity to the Tri-Cities. The 1910 census showed Davenport as the second-richest city per capita in the United States. High employment put more money into corporate, city and private pocketbooks than was needed for necessities, resulting in grander buildings, spruced-up downtowns, and a flourishing of entertainment and the arts. Rock Island opened two new parks, Longview Park (carved out of 40 acres of Bailey Davenport's pasture in 1908) and Lincoln Park (opened in 1909,

RIGHT *LEON "BIX" BEIDERBECKE, THE FAMOUS JAZZ CORNET PLAYER, WAS BORN AND RAISED IN DAVENPORT. HE ACHIEVED FAME WITH MANY DIFFERENT BANDS THROUGHOUT THE 1920s WITH POPULAR TUNES, INCLUDING "DAVENPORT BLUES" AND "IN THE DARK." BEIDERBECKE DIED IN 1931 AS A RESULT OF PNEUMONIA AND ALCOHOLISM AT THE YOUNG AGE OF TWENTY-EIGHT.*

FAR RIGHT *ALICE FRENCH, WHO WROTE UNDER THE PEN NAME OCTAVE THANET, WAS THE ELDER STATESWOMAN OF THE LOCAL LITERARY RENAISSANCE OF THE EARLY 20TH CENTURY. MANY OF HER STORIES, WHICH APPEARED IN NATIONAL MAGAZINES, WERE SET IN DAVENPORT.*

CENTER RIGHT *AN INEXPENSIVE FORM OF ENTERTAINMENT COULD BE FOUND AT THE DAVENPORT LIBRARY. ANDREW CARNEGIE DONATED $75,000 TO THE CONSTRUCTION OF A LIBRARY FOR THE CITY OF DAVENPORT IN 1900. THIS HELPED TO BUILD THE LIBRARY WHICH WAS DEDICATED IN 1904. THE CHILDREN'S ROOM OF THE LIBRARY IS SHOWN HERE.*

BELOW LEFT *SUSAN GLASPELL WAS ONE OF SEVERAL NATIONALLY PROMINENT WRITERS FROM DAVENPORT. SHE GRADUATED FROM DAVENPORT HIGH SCHOOL IN 1893 AND PUBLISHED HER FIRST SHORT STORY TEN YEARS LATER. IN 1931, GLASPELL WON THE PULITZER PRIZE FOR DRAMA WITH HER WORK,* ALISON'S HOUSE.

BELOW RIGHT *THE PROSPERITY OF THE EARLY 20TH CENTURY BROUGHT A NUMBER OF CULTURAL INTERESTS TO THE TRI-CITIES. THE TRI-CITIES SYMPHONY WAS FOUNDED IN 1914 AND BECAME THE QUAD CITY SYMPHONY IN 1985. THIS PHOTO WAS TAKEN DURING A RADIO BROADCAST AT THE MASONIC TEMPLE.*

Courtesy, Davenport Public Library.

Courtesy, Davenport Public Library.

Courtesy, Davenport Public Library.

Courtesy, Davenport Public Library.

Courtesy, Davenport Public Library.

Courtesy, Putnam Museum. *Courtesy, Davenport Public Library.*

Courtesy, Augustana College Library, Special Collections.

annual Bix Beiderbecke Memorial Jazz Festival in Davenport beginning in 1972.

Labor

The success of the large corporation had a price. In the early 20th century Tri-Cities, that price was paid by labor. Before the Civil War, the westward movement of immigrants had provided ideal conditions for both employee and employer: a plentiful supply of workers who could stop to work if there was work or move on if there was not. In the more settled landscape after the war, workers found themselves captives of the economy.

As early as 1868, craft unions such as the Coachmaker's International and the Tailor's Association had organized in the Tri-Cities, followed by the larger Knights of Labor in 1882 and the Tri-City Labor Congress in 1886. Although there were strikes such as that at the Kuhnen Cigar Company in 1882, these 19th century craft unions were more interested in improving the lot of the worker through education and socialization. Labor Day was first celebrated in 1889 in the Tri-Cities.

The large corporation and the complexity of the new equipment manufactured both helped to depersonalize the workplace. From the small machine shop where the owner worked alongside employees to a corporation where the chairman of the board sat distant from the worker who was hired and fired, and from crafting an entire product to standing at a work station repeating a single action, workers now found themselves isolated.

They also found themselves more at risk. Many of the new automated assembly line jobs did not require skilled, trained workers, and therefore did not command as high wages. Such workers were easily replaced by others willing to work for less. In the Tri-Cities, as elsewhere, that often meant immigrants, and waves of Belgians and Greeks now joined the Swedes and Germans who were still arriving to work in local factories.

Labor organizations adapted to represent this new worker by moving to a concern with working conditions and the economics of the workplace. In 1894, workers from 32 trade unions marched on the Davenport mayor's office to demand work. Strikes increased after the turn of the century, with major trouble at Root and VanderVoort Engineering and at the Deere-Clark Motor Company in 1907. As unions grew more militant and politically radical (the International Workers of the World organized in Chicago in 1905), employers stiffened their resistance with lockouts, blacklists, and strikebreakers--the beginning of a long history of antagonism in local labor relations.

Although unions were not the norm until well into the 20th century, labor unions in the Tri-Cities had risen to a membership of 7,000 by 1911, the year the *Tri-City Labor Review* newspaper began publication. A strong labor voice was partly responsible for placing socialist candidates on the Davenport City Council prior to the 1920s. In 1921 Davenport elected a socialist city administration in a landslide victory for its candidate, Dr. C. L. Barewald.

World War I

Along with much of the Midwest, the Tri-Cities resisted the United States' gradual involvement in the War in Europe between 1914 and 1917, but the threat of war was particularly hard on Davenport's Germans. Their support of the Civil War had made them respected members of the community, but that good will now disappeared. Many Davenport Germans had relatives in Germany, and themselves wavered in their loyalties. Support for the German side in some of their local publications helped fuel anti-German sentiment. As a result the Tri-Cities fought a war on the home front as well as in Europe. Davenport's Harrison Street became known as the Hindenberg Line, and the German area to the northwest as Sauerkraut Hill. Anti-German groups such as the

Scott County Protective Association goaded some residents to paint the doors of German homes yellow and to desecrate statues in Washington Square. The Davenport Public Library discontinued collections of German newspapers and magazines. Iowa Governor William Harding added to the conflict by forbidding the use of all foreign languages in public speeches, publications, schools, and churchs in Iowa. Anti-German sentiment erased much of the visible Germanness in the Tri-Cities. The German Savings Bank in Davenport became the American Commercial Bank, and on September 7, 1918, *Der Demokrat*, the newspaper begun in 1851, published its last issue.

The distant war came home in other ways, too. On March 27, 1918, Marion Crandell, a French teacher at St. Katherine's School in Davenport who had joined the Red Cross, became the first American woman to die in active service when she was killed in heavy bombing at St. Menehould. Those who stayed at home held thrift shop sales and Liberty Loan campaigns. Groups known as "Sammie's Helpers" made bandages, while local schools added Spanish, French, and telegraphy to their curricula.

At the Rock Island Arsenal, the production of war materiel pushed employment from less that 2,000 to a peak of 14,778 in November of 1918. To protect Arsenal workers, the Government decreed that "all saloons and bawdy houses within a half mile of the Rock Island Arsenal must close within 36 hours," a ruling that closed 48 bars in Bucktown alone, virtually eliminating that notorious riverfront area.

World War I brought a new immigrant group to the Tri-Cities. To ease a shortage of workers at the Bettendorf Company, William Bettendorf traveled to Juarez, Mexico, where he recruited 150 men. For them, and for their wives and children who followed, Bettendorf built a small ghetto of apartments and one-

EVANGELIST BILLY SUNDAY CAME TO ROCK ISLAND FOR SEVERAL WEEKS IN SEPTEMBER OF 1919. SUNDAY'S CRUSADE GAINED OVER 10,000 CONVERTS. THIS WAS ALSO A RETURN HOME FOR SUNDAY; WHEN HE WAS A CHILD, HE SPENT THREE YEARS IN THE IOWA SOLDIERS' ORPHANS' HOME.

Courtesy, Rock Island County Historical Society.

room cottages near the plant—an area that came to be known as Holy City, ostensibly from the fact that so many workers signed the company role as "Jesus." The Rock Island Lines also imported Mexican labor for the Silvis Shops, where a lack of housing forced many of them to live in abandoned company box cars and even hold the services of Our Lady of Guadalupe in two box cars from 1927-30.

The Roaring Twenties

The Armistice on November 11, 1918, brought peace and a respite for Davenport Germans, but a new enemy was in the wings. The Prohibition Amendment was not well observed in the Tri-Cities, where the many islands in the river provided ideal sites for stills and storage. Prohibition, in conflict with new liberal moral values, set the stage for a battle.

In the post-war fight between good and evil, both sides brought big guns to bear. On the side of good were evangelists such as Billy Sunday, who came to Rock Island for several weeks in September of 1919. In an 8,000-seat tabernacle constructed just for his crusade, Sunday preached to 20,000 people in three services on the opening day, and by the end, had made 10,612 converts. For Billy Sunday, this was a return home. Earlier, his widowed mother had put him and a brother in the Iowa Soldiers' Orphans' Home for three years.

On the side of evil was a notorious Rock Islander, John Looney. In 1905 Looney began publishing the *Rock Island News*, a "moral newspaper" he called it, standing for "Truth, Good Government, and the Protection of the People." In fact, Looney used the paper to shake down prominent people, who paid to keep from seeing themselves in such headlines as "Managing Editor of the *Argus* Paroled From The

Crazy House At Watertown." A Looney-created riot in Market Square in 1912 killed two bystanders and forced Illinois Governor Charles Deneen to declare martial law and bring in the National Guard to enforce a curfew in Rock Island. On October 26, 1922, Looney's son, Connor, was gunned down in front of the Sherman Hotel by four gunmen in two cars, marking the beginning of a rapid decline in Looney fortunes.

By then, Rock Island had already lost caste. Tri-Citians forgot that Bishop Henry Cosgrove in 1903 had called Davenport "the wickedest city for its size in America" and passed that reputation on to Rock Island.

Neither good nor evil prevented the Tri-Cities from experiencing another economic boom in the 1920s. In 1927, Robinson's Hardware opened in Rock Island, the Dewey Portland Cement Company opened southwest of Davenport, and Royal Neighbors of America opened a new headquarters in Rock Island, preparatory to becoming separate from Modern Woodman in 1929, the same year the new Bituminous Insurance built its corporate headquarters. Between 1927 and 1929, fifteen new businesses opened in Davenport, including the Victor Animatographic Company, a developer of sixteen milimeter home movie equipment.

The Kahl Building (1920), the Parker Building (1922) companion to the Putnam Building, and modern hotels such as the LeClaire in Moline (1926), the Fort Armstrong in Rock Island (1926), the Hotel Davenport (1907) and the Black Hawk in Davenport (1915) helped to give the downtowns a more metropolitan look. Spectacular new movie palaces such as the Fort Theater in Rock Island (1921) and the Capitol in Davenport (1920) dwarfed the earlier small neighborhood theaters.

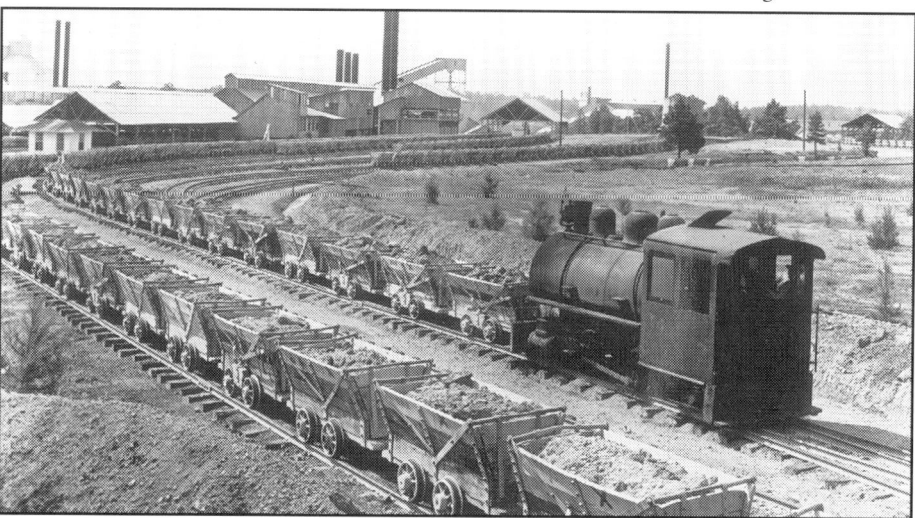

THE DEWEY PORTLAND CEMENT COMPANY OPENED SOUTHWEST OF DAVENPORT IN 1927. THIS VIEW SHOWS CARTS BEING PUSHED TO THE CEMENT PLANT FROM THE QUARRY.

Courtesy, Davenport Public Library.

Courtesy, Davenport Public Library.

Courtesy, Rock Island County Historical Society.

Courtesy, Putnam Museum.

Movies were shortly joined by a new media. In 1922, B. J. Palmer bought a local amateur radio station, WOC, and moved it to the Brady Street hill near Palmer College of Chiropractic. WOC was the first station west of the Mississippi and the second licensed station in the United States. A Rock Island radio buff, Calvin Beardsley, went on the air for four hours a week from the back of the Beardsley Specialty Company in 1925 as WHBF (a contest-winning entry standing for Where Historic Blackhawk Fought). In 1932 WHBF was sold to the John W. Potter Company, publishers of the *Rock Island Argus*.

Although local residents like to tell visitors that Ronald Reagan briefly worked as a part-time sports announcer for WOC in 1932, a more important Tri-Cities contribution to radio was Charles Correll's. Correll came to Rock Island in 1912 as a bricklayer. In 1928, Correll and a partner, Freeman Gosden, thought up the idea for *Amos 'n' Andy*. Nightly from 1928 until 1943, Correll played Andy on a program so popular that movie theaters often stopped the movie for the fifteen minute broadcast.

As radio programs filled the airwaves, the flying field became a new feature of the landscape. Tri-Citians were fascinated with the flying machine, and several played a part in its development. On September 14, at the 9th Street fairgrounds in Rock Island, a crowd of 5,000 watched Davenporter, Lieutenant Eugene Ely, make the first successful flight between St. Paul and St. Louis. Two months later, Lt. Ely made the world's first flight from the deck of a ship.

By 1919, the first airport, Franing Field, had appeared in a Rock River valley pasture south of Moline, followed by an airfield east of downtown Moline on 23rd Avenue, and by Cram Field on Division Street in Davenport (1928) named for Ralph Cram, the "Flying Editor" of the *Davenport Democrat*. Franing Field became the present Quad City Airport.

Of all the Tri-Cities' contributions to aviation, none was more important than the Velie Monocoupe. Two young Bettendorf aviation enthusiasts, Don Luscombe and Clayton Folkerts, organized the

Central States Aero Company and designed an enclosed cabin monoplane in 1926, powered with the Velie 5-cylinder engine. Their request for a more powerful Velie engine led to a partnership known as the Mono Aircraft Corporation, a subsidiary of the Velie Motor Company. A year later, at the 1928 National Air Races in Los Angeles, Velie Monocoupes won a number of closed course events against more powerful aircraft. In 1929, Phoebe Omlie established a world altitude record for women in a Velie Monocoupe over the Tri-Cities.

The deaths of Willard Velie and his son sent the manufacturing operation to become part of Allied Aviation in St. Louis, but the enclosed cabin of the Velie plane and its dependable Velie engine marked the beginnings of the light plane industry in the United States.

The Great Depression

The stockmarket crash on October 29, 1929, had little immediate effect on the growth that had

Courtesy, Davenport Public Library.

THE 2,700-SEAT RKO ORPHEUM THEATER OPENED IN 1931 AS PART OF THE $2 MILLION MISSISSIPPI HOTEL COMPLEX IN DOWNTOWN DAVENPORT. THIS CREATIVE LOBBY DISPLAY PROMOTED THE NEW FRANCIS, THE TALKING MULE FILM OF 1950, "FRANCIS GOES TO THE RACES."

Couresty, Davenport Public Library.

characterized the first three decades of the 20th century. In 1929, a Montgomery Wards store brought a new form of merchandizing to Davenport. Both Sears and J. C. Penny followed Wards in 1930, part of a building boom in Davenport that ranked it that year among the top 20 cities in the United States. In Moline, the eight-story, art deco Fifth Avenue Building opened in 1930, influenced by the 1925 Paris Exposition.

By the time the grand new 2,700-seat RKO Orpheum Theater opened in 1931 as part of the $2,000,000 Mississippi Hotel complex, there was trouble. By 1931, the Bettendorf Company had closed, on the brink of bankruptcy. In 1932, 7,000 people a month were getting relief payments in Scott County. Soup kitchens appeared, as did shelters such as F. W. Donaway's Rock Island Rescue Mission. By the end of 1932, the six Deere plants on the Illinois

ABOVE LEFT ANOTHER CIVIL WORKS ADMINISTRATION UNDERTAKING WAS THE RE-LAYING OF BRICKS ON EAST RIVER DRIVE IN DAVENPORT. THIS PHOTO SHOWS MEN WORKING IN FRONT OF THE WONDER BREAD BAKERY NEAR ONEIDA STREET IN 1934.

LEFT DURING THE 1936 ELECTION CAMPAIGN, PRESIDENT FRANKLIN ROOSEVELT AND FIRST LADY ELEANOR ROOSEVELT VISITED THE QUAD CITIES. MANY QUAD CITIANS FOUND EMPLOYMENT THROUGH ROOSEVELT'S WORKS PROJECTS ADMINISTRATION. ROOSEVELT'S CAMPAIGN TRAIN STOPPED IN DAVENPORT WHERE HE PROUDLY DISPLAYED IOWA'S STAPLE CROP.

Courtesy, Davenport Public Library.

ABOVE *DURING THE GREAT DEPRESSION, MANY UNEMPLOYED WORKERS FOUND JOBS FUNDED BY THE WORKS PROJECTS ADMINISTRATION UNDER THE NATIONAL RECOVERY ACT. ONE SUCH PROJECT WAS THE IOWA-ILLINOIS MEMORIAL SUSPENSION BRIDGE BETWEEN BETTENDORF AND MOLINE BUILT IN 1935.*

ABOVE RIGHT *THE MOLINE LOCK WAS BUILT AT THE FOOT OF BENHAM'S ISLAND NEAR THE EASTERN TIP OF ARSENAL ISLAND. THIS LOCK AND CANAL WAS INTENDED TO PROVIDE MOLINE WITH A HARBOR FOR ITS FACTORIES.*

CENTER RIGHT *THE HENNEPIN CANAL, ALSO KNOWN AS THE ILLINOIS AND MISSISSIPPI CANAL, OPENED IN 1907. THE OFFICER IN CHARGE OF THE CANAL EXPERIMENTED WITH POURED CONCETE LOCK WALLS INSTEAD OF TRADITIONAL MASONRY CONSTRUCTION. THIS TECHNIQUE DRASTICALLY IMPROVED THE AMERICAN CONSTRUCTION INDUSTRY AND HELPED MAKE THE BUILDING OF THE PANAMA CANAL POSSIBLE.*

LOWER RIGHT *WHEN THE IOWA-ILLINOIS MEMORIAL BRIDGE OPENED IN 1935, TOLL BOOTHS WERE USED TO HELP PAY FOR THE CONSTRUCTION. THE BRIDGE'S TOLL OPERATORS ARE PICTURED HERE SHORTLY AFTER THE BRIDGE OPENED.*

LEFT *THE PALMER COLLEGE OF CHIROPRACTIC IS SHOWN HERE IN THE 1940s. THE SCHOOL IS STILL LOCATED AT THE TOP OF BRADY STREET HILL IN DAVENPORT.*

LOWER LEFT *BETWEEN 1931 AND 1939, THE U.S. ARMY CORPS OF ENGINEERS BUILT TWENTY-SIX LOCKS AND DAMS ON THE UPPER MISSISSIPPI. THE FIRST OF THESE WAS LOCK AND DAM 15, SHOWN HERE DWARFING SOME CONSTUCTION WORKERS, AT THE FOOT OF THE ROCK ISLAND RAPIDS BETWEEN ARSENAL ISLAND AND DAVENPORT.*

LOWER RIGHT *ROCK ISLAND CELEBRATED ITS OWN CENTENNIAL IN 1941 BY OPENING THE CENTENNIAL BRIDGE BETWEEN ROCK ISLAND AND DAVENPORT. THIS PHOTO SHOWS THE DAVENPORT TURNER GIRLS MARCHING BAND PERFORMING AT THE DEDICATION CEREMONY FOR THE CENTENNIAL BRIDGE.*

Courtesy, Augustana College Library, Special Collections.

Courtesy, Augustana College Library, Special Collections.

side employed only 716. Fifty companies closed in 1933.

Banks were especially vulnerable. Of the few that survived, none had as dramatic a rescue as that of Davenport's American Commercial Savings Bank. When a run developed at the bank in 1931, E. P. Adler, publisher of the *Davenport Daily Times*, appeared and personally guaranteed depositors' money. He then put together a reorganization plan and served as the unpaid president while he brought in as executive vice-president a young bank examiner named V. O. Figge. The bank reopened on July 5, 1932. It became Davenport Bank and Trust, and under Figge's hands-on, conservative methods,

showed 57 years of annual earning increases.

Many displaced workers found themselves working on large federal, state, and local projects funded by the Works Progress Administration under the National Recovery Act. In Davenport, these included a municipal stadium (named John O'Donnell Stadium in 1970) along the riverfront and the Iowa-Illinois Memorial suspension bridge between Bettendorf and Moline. Federal funds also built the U. S. Outerbelt Highway on the north side of Davenport (renamed Kimberly Road in 1936). In Moline, the creation of a 205-acre municipal airport out of Franing Field became the largest WPA project in Illinois. Rock Island benefitted by a new National

Guard armory in 1937, a new city hall, and a new Rock Island High School.

Of all the Government projects which boosted local economy, however, none provided as many jobs as the 9-foot river channel authorized by Congress in 1930. Previous attempts to improve river transportation had included the Illinois and Mississippi Canal between the mouth of the Rock River and Hennepin on the Illinois River, opened in 1907, and the Moline Lock at the foot of Benham's Island near the eastern tip of Arsenal Island, intended to provide river access for the Moline factories, in 1905.

Both projects fell far short of expectations, but they produced an unexpected benefit. Captain W. L. Marshall, the officer in charge of the Hennepin Canal, received permission to experiment with poured concrete lock walls instead of using traditional masonry construction. The machinery he invented to mix and pour such large batches of concrete, and his use of American (Portland) cement rather than imported varieties, revolutionized the American construction industry and helped make possible the building of the Panama Canal. The Safety Building in Rock Island in 1908 was among the first in the country to use the new poured concrete construction

The 9-foot channel was a radical departure from previous projects which left the channel open. Between 1931 and 1939, the Corps of Engineers and hundreds of subcontractors turned the Upper Mississippi into an "aquatic staircase" with 26 locks and dams. The first of these was Lock and Dam 15 at the foot of the rapids between Arsenal Island and Davenport, begun in 1931 and opened to traffic in 1934. The last lock and dam in the project, Number 14 at LeClaire in 1939, submerged the Rock Island Rapids forever.

These Federal projects spurred local industries to aid in the recovery. By 1934, employment at the Deere and Company shops had climbed to 2,200. International Harvester poured large sums of money into the Farmall plant in Rock Island until employment reached 5,000 by 1939. A new farm equipment business arrived in 1937 when J. I. Case bought the old Rock Island Plow Company, turning out a new tractor line with 1,000 employees by 1939. Servus Rubber which had opened in 1923 expanded to a full capacity of 1,000 workers by 1940. Rock Island celebrated the end of the Depression, and its own centennial in 1941 by opening the Centennial Bridge between Rock Island and Davenport.

World War II

Few people old enough to remember have forgotten where they were on that cold, bright Sunday afternoon of December 7, 1941. In Rock Island, many were watching Gary Cooper in *Sergeant York* at the Fort Armstrong matinee or Andy Rooney and Judy Garland in *Life Begins for Andy Hardy* at the Spencer.

If Pearl Harbor shocked Tri-Citians, the coming of the war did not. Few could avoid noticing the increased activity at the Arsenal. Following America's unspoken decision to become the "arsenal of democracy," the shops at Rock Island added new buildings and equipment to manufacture artillery vehicles, .30 calibre machine guns, and many smaller parts. By 1939, local businesses were under private contract to manufacture war items. The Crescent Bakery in Davenport made C-rations; Servus Rubber in Rock Island turned out waterproof boots and tents; in Moline, Williams, White & Company manufactured hydraulic presses for aviation companies and Moline Forge made 7mm artillery projectiles. Deere and Company made small machine parts as well as transmissions and final drive units for the M3 Tank. During the war, Farmall shipped thousands of tractors to lend-lease countries, while J. I. Case manufactured 111,000 500-pound bombs.

Employment at the Arsenal rose to a peak of 18,675 workers in 1943, with more than 90,000 people at work in local industry. The demand for workers changed the nature of employment. Arsenal recruiters went door-to-door to find anyone able to work. For the first time, significant numbers of women, minorities, and the handicapped entered a workplace previously closed to them. By 1944, 32% of the Arsenal workers were women, as were 37% of the workers in local shops.

As it had during World War I, the Government built housing for the flood of new workers. One of the major projects was Arsenal Courts, 305 low-rental apartment units in Rock Island's west end. Because the Arsenal recruited numbers of blacks from the South, and because these out-of-town workers had little choice but to live in Arsenal Courts, and because employment at the Arsenal dropped quickly after the war, the Arsenal inadvertently played a part in turning the west end of Rock Island into a ghetto of high unemployment.

World War I had ended with the euphoria of having made the world safe for democracy; the celebrations at the end of World War II were more problematic. The uncertainties of an atomic future were heightened by uncertainties of the workplace. The world to come held out both new horizons and storm clouds.

CHAPTER FIVE:

Post-War Prosperity 1945-1960

LATE IN 1945, LOOKING FORWARD TO A RENEWED BUSINESS CLIMATE, THE DAVENPORT CHAMBER OF COMMERCE LAUNCHED A "THOUSAND DAYS Program," an advertising campaign to show the world the advantages of the Quad Cities' climate, natural resources, entertainment and skilled workforce. The campaign worked. In 1946 alone, Oscar Mayer took over the Kohn Packing Company in Davenport, the Curtis-Wright Corporation bought out Victor Animatographic with plans to expand, and Lusk/Fresh Pak Candy was founded in Davenport. By the end of the thousand days in 1948, Davenport had developed a new industrialized area in the west end, with such companies as Red Jacket Manufacturing, Ralston Purina, Nichols Wire and Aluminum, Priester Construction, Independent Biscuit, and a Giefman grocery chain warehouse.

In addition, the campaign brought two major industries to Scott County. In 1946, the Aluminum Company of America began construction of the world's largest aluminum rolling mill on a 400 acre site along the Mississippi just east of Bettendorf, with plans for a workforce of 2,000. The following year, J. I. Case moved into the old Bettendorf Car Works.

The immensity of the Alcoa operation led to the

Courtesy, Davenport Public Library.

THE ALUMINUM COMPANY OF AMERICA, OR ALCOA, BEGAN CONSTRUCTION OF THE WORLD'S LARGEST ALUMINUM ROLLING MILL ALONG THE MISSISSIPPI JUST EAST OF BETTENDORF IN 1946. THIS PHOTO SHOWS TWO ALCOA EMPLOYEES AMONG THE STACKS OF ALUMINUM SHEETS.

formation of a new town. Already pressed for space and aware of the tax base Alcoa represented, Bettendorf began annexation proceedings of the land surrounding the new plant in the summer of 1950. With the encouragement of Alcoa, property owners in the vicinity of the Alcoa plant headed off annexation with a petition to incorporate a 2 1/2-square mile area from Duck Creek east as the town of Riverdale, a move confirmed by a vote of 112 to 3 in November. Alcoa's location within the corporate limits gave the new community an assessed valuation greater than any other town in Iowa.

Across the river, industries were also recovering from wartime shortages and restrictions with rapid growth. Case added on to its Rock Island plant in 1946, and in 1947, International Harvester constructed a block-long addition to the Farmall Works. This expansion of both new and existing industries

Courtesy, Davenport Public Library.

THE VICTOR ANIMATOGRAPHIC COMPANY OPENED IN THE LATE 1920S. THE COMPANY DEVELOPED SIXTEEN MILLIMETER HOME MOVIE EQUIPMENT LIKE THESE FILM PROJECTORS BEING ASSEMBLED. VICTOR ANIMATOGRAPHIC WAS BOUGHT OUT IN 1946 BY THE CURTIS-WRIGHT CORPORATION.

THE DEAR JOES WERE WELCOMED HOME FROM WORLD WAR II BY EVERYONE, INCLUDING DAVENPORT MAYOR ARTHUR R. KROPPACH, DURING THE FIRST ANNUAL "STATE OF SCOTT" CELEBRATION. DEAR JOE WAS ORIGINALLY A CREATION OF SPORTS COLUMNIST, JOHN O'DONNELL, WHO WROTE A LETTER IN ONE OF HIS COLUMNS TO A MYTHICAL "DEAR JOE" AT THE FRONT. QUAD CITY SOLDIERS RESPONDED UNTIL DEAR JOE CORRESPONDENCE FILLED TWO PAGES EACH SUNDAY.

was made possible in great part by a skilled workforce trained at the Arsenal and at other war production facilities who were now suddenly available as the Arsenal reduced employment from more than 23,000 during the war to less than 6,000 in 1945, and to half of that in 1946.

In addition, there were hundreds of returning G.I.s, or Dear Joes as they were known in the Quad Cities. Dear Joe was originally a creation of *Davenport Democrat* sports columnist John O'Donnell, who wrote a letter in one of his columns to a mythical "Dear Joe" at the front. Quad City soldiers responded until Dear Joe correspondence filled two pages each Sunday. O'Donnell had captured something of the mood and feeling of Quad Citians. Soldiers used the column to keep in touch with each other.

The Dear Joes were formally welcomed home in June 1946, during the first annual "State of Scott" celebration. "Dear Joes: Welcome!" read the headlines of the *Democrat*. The heart of this celebration, which included an elected governor, an air show, and five inaugural balls throughout Davenport, were the members of the Dear Joe Club, who presented John O'Donnell with a new Hudson.

The Dear Joes swelled the ranks of the American Legion, leading to a new Legion building on the Davenport levee in 1950, but underneath the joy of their return lay disturbing questions. The veterans were returning with new values and expectations, eager to make up for lost time, and they were returning to jobs that had been filled by women and minorities, who now feared they would lose those jobs.

Housing was in critically short supply, prices of food and other necessities soared with the lifting of price controls, and the ending of wartime regulation of the workplace left both workers and managers suspicious of each other. The late 1940s, therefore, turned out to be an uncertain and uncomfortable period of adjustment for the Quad Cities.

Much of that adjustment took visible form as labor unrest, a series of long and sometimes violent strikes. The displacement of workers as veterans returned to their jobs was only one of the problems. Plants which had worked heavy overtime during the war now cut back hours, resulting in an average loss of take-home pay in the Quad Cities of some 30%. In addition, a number of grievances on the part of both labor and management, hidden by the war, had been building. Unions seeking more power met a growing employer resistance to unions. Workers themselves, facing a future whose direction was hard to predict, expanded their demands from a concentration on wages before the war to new areas such as pensions, cost-of-living adjustments, insurance, and health care. A strike at the Dewey Portland Cement Company just after the war ended was followed by many others. A violent 65-day strike at J. I. Case erupted in December of 1945, followed by a protracted 85-day strike at the Farmall Plant early in January. Passage of the Taft-Hartley Act in 1947, curtailing the rights of unions to strike, increased the tension between labor and management in the Quad Cities and led to additional strikes. The 110-day strike at Deere and Company in 1950 (longest in the nation that year and longest ever in the Quad Cities)

Courtesy, The Children's Museum Foundation.

Courtesy, The Children's Museum Foundation.

MANY LABOR STRIKES TOOK PLACE IN THE QUAD CITIES IN 1950. BY SEPTEMBER OF THAT YEAR, 14,000 WORKERS IN THE QUAD CITIES WERE ON STRIKE AT THE SAME TIME. THE LOSS OF JOBS FROM THE LOCKOUTS, AND SHUTDOWNS GROWING OUT OF THESE STRIKES MADE 1950 A PEAK YEAR FOR POST-WAR UNEMPLOYMENT. THE TWO VIEWS SHOW SOME OF THE OUTBREAKS OF VIOLENCE DURING SEPTEMBER OF 1950.

was only one of many that strife-ridden year during which seven farm equipment plants were idled. Strikes at the American Container Corporation and the Rock Island Lines, and by ironworkers, sheetmetal workers, and telephone equipment installers swelled the numbers. By September of 1950, 14,000 workers in the Quad Cities were on strike at the same time. The loss of jobs from the lockouts and shutdowns growing out of these strikes made 1950 a peak year for post-war unemployment.

Some of the most violent labor troubles in the Quad Cities arose not out of disagreements between union and management but from confrontations between rival unions competing to organize the farm equipment industry through differing ideologies and tactics. The older American Federation of Labor was a conservative organization that limited its membership to skilled workers grouped by craft or occupation. In the 1930s, a struggle within the AFL over these issues led to the formation of a Committee for Industrial Organization, which soon became

Courtesy, The Dispatch/The Rock Island Argus.

independent organization under John L. Lewis. The CIO wanted to organize all workers in mass production industries, including the farm equipment plants in the Quad Cities. By the end of World War II, the CIO's United Farm Equipment Workers had organized Deere and International Harvester. However, another CIO union, the United Auto Workers, had organized J. I. Case plants and wanted to take over all farm equipment workers in a single union for better bargaining. The year 1947 marked the beginning of a struggle between these two unions. Using militant tactics including wildcat strikes, fist fights, and other violent acts which resulted in the arrest of many workers, the UFE began pressing International Harvester in Rock Island and East Moline. These activities in February became the subject of a Con-

gressional hearing in Washington, partly because the UFE was suspected of communist infiltration, but they were successful in obtaining a new contract at IH by 1948.

In October of 1949, the UFE merged with the United Electrical Workers, and that November, the combined union was expelled from the CIO because of alleged communist ties at the top. In 1952, the UE-FE called a strike at IH against the wishes of the workers. For this reason, and also because IH publicized its opposition as a moral crusade against communism, the strike collapsed. It was the failure of this strike at IH that led to the eventual absorption of the UE-FE by the rival UAW, who by now had won the right to organize many local industries, including all seven Deere plants.

In 1955, the AFL and CIO, divested of their more radical elements, merged. This, and the beginning of collective bargaining in the Quad Cities, calmed the tension between labor and management, and helped create a decade of prosperity for both manufacturing concerns and for local communities.

Meanwhile, outside the workplace, the Quad Cities was also adjusting to post-war America. New entertainments, new living arrangements, new housing patterns, and new cars rapidly changed both the landscape of the cities themselves and the expectations of the people who lived there.

One of the first casualties of these changes was gambling. Gambling had been a part of Quad City culture as least since the sawmill days following the

Courtesy, Augustana College Library, Special Collections.

Civil War; it continued to thrive through the Roaring Twenties and World War II. Following the war, it exploded into nearly every bar and into many of the larger and fancier restaurants and nightclubs in Scott and Rock Island counties. Everything from punchboards and jars-of-fun to slot machines and high stakes cards flourished amid sporadic police raids. That is, until 1948, when a determined young Moline woman, Marie Van Muelbrock, launched a personal crusade. Van Muelbrock visited dozens of bars, sometimes with her mother and sister, calling the police when she found gambling and remaining on site until they arrived to make sure there was an arrest. Late in 1948, after serving a jail sentence for throwing a brick through a bar window, and gaining national attention as "the Joan of Arc against gambling," Van Muelbrock found an ally in a newly-elected Rock Island County States Attorney, Bernard J. Moran,

who launched a wholesale crackdown in Rock Island County. A single campaign in August of 1950 netted 1,293 violations. Although bingo games continued to appear, disguised as ice cream socials, Moran's efforts and a new anti-gambling law in Iowa in 1951, effectively ended the wide open gambling that had characterized the Old Tri-Cities.

Quad Citians did not have long to wait for a new addiction. WHBF-TV began limited broadcasting in the spring of 1949 to some 1,750 television sets in the Quad Cities. WOC-TV became Iowa's first television station the following October, with a daily evening program consisting of the *Kukla, Fran and Ollie* puppet show followed by a movie. By the time WHBF-TV received its commercial licence in 1951– the first in Illinois outside of Chicago–there were 85,000 sets in use.

Courtesy, Davenport Public Library.

Courtesy, Davenport Public Library.

Courtesy, Davenport Public Library.

ABOVE LEFT *DAVENPORT MUNICIPAL STADIUM, LATER NAMED JOHN O'DONNELL STADIUM, OPENED ALONG THE RIVERFRONT IN 1931. THE STADIUM WAS HOME TO A NUMBER OF DIFFERENT TEAMS. THE CHICAGO CUBS' FARM TEAM BEGAN PLAY HERE IN 1947 AND THE QUAD-CITY QUADS PLAYED HERE FOR A FEW SEASONS STARTING IN 1950. IN RECENT YEARS, THE STADIUM UNDERWENT MASSIVE RENOVATIONS AND TODAY THE QUAD-CITY RIVER BANDITS CALL THE STADIUM HOME.*

ABOVE RIGHT *JACK FLECK WAS GIVEN A HERO'S WELCOME WHEN HE RETURNED HOME AFTER WINNING GOLF'S U.S. OPEN IN 1955. HE DEFEATED THE LEGENDARY BEN HOGAN IN A PLAYOFF TO WIN THE TITLE.*

LEFT *THE GOLDEN OPPORTUNITY SHOW FEATURED LOCAL TALENT ON WOC-TV IN DAVENPORT. MARJORIE MEINERT WAS THE ORGANIST AND WARREN VASSEN HOSTED THE PROGRAM. THIS VIEW SHOWS A GROUP OF YOUNG WOMEN SHOWING OFF THEIR ACCORDIAN SKILLS.*

The first television programs were supplied by the network, but extensive local programing soon created the first Quad Cities television personalities. WOC viewers came to know former beauty queen and model, Pat Sundine, through her half-hour homemaking show five days a week, organist Marjorie Meinert, and Warren Vassen, host of the *Golden Opportunity Show* featuring local talent. Adults watched the local game show, *Scramblegrams*, while children kept busy after school watching *Cap'n Vern's Cartoon Showboat*, or his competitor across the river at WHBF, Grandpa Happy.

Not all eyes were glued to television sets. Radio stations proliferated, too, including Moline's first AM station, WQUA, in 1947. Arts, music, and sports kept up a long tradition in the Quad Cities of supporting local amateur groups as well as professionals from outside. In 1947, a professional basketball team, the Blackhawks, playing for the National Basketball League, debuted in Moline's Wharton Field House. That same year, the Chicago Cubs' farm team began playing at the Davenport Municipal Stadium, while the Philadephia Athletics sponsored the Moline Athletics of the new Central Baseball Association. Davenport's own baseball team, the Quad-City Quads, began playing in 1950 and lasted for several seasons. An increased interest in golf after the war was capped by Davenporter Jack Fleck's winning of the 1955 U. S. Open in a playoff with the legendary golf great, Ben Hogan.

Music, art, and theater also flourished in the heady environment of the post-war Quad Cities. Marando's Supper Club in Milan opened in 1948 and

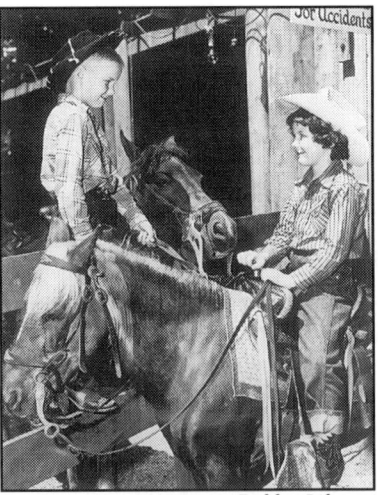

THE CHILDREN'S ZOO AT FEJERVARY PARK IN DAVENPORT OPENED IN THE SUMMER OF 1953. THE PARK INCLUDED MONKEY ISLAND WITH RHESUS MONKEYS AND ALSO PONY RIDES. THIS YOUNG BOY AND GIRL WERE SHOWN GETTING READY FOR THEIR PONY RIDE.

Courtesy, Davenport Public Library.

continued a tradition begun by the old Burtis Opera House and the Harper Hotel of bringing big-name entertainment to local audiences. In 1949, the Quad City Music Guild began putting on a summer season of musicals at Prospect Park in Moline. At about the same time, a music teacher at John Deere Junior High in Moline, Fred Swanson, organized the Moline Boys Choir and directed it to national prominence. In Davenport, a theater legend, Mary F. Nighswander, returned after a successful stage career to help found the Davenport Junior Theater, giving young people a change to appear on stage. In 1956, a WHBF employee, Don Wooten, organized the Genesius Guild to put on free summer plays in Rock Island's Lincoln Park. The Genesius Guild has become a legend for its productions of Shakespeare and Greek drama. Over the years, faithful Lincoln Park audiences have seen a more extensive repertoire of classical Greek tragedies and comedies than they could have seen in any other single location. In 1959, another local theater group, the Playcrafters, moved into a permanent home, the Barn Theater, in Moline to perform popular stage plays.

The first two area zoos appeared during these postwar years. In the summer of 1953, a children's zoo opened at Fejevary Park in Davenport, and in 1959, Gordon McLain opened his Wildlife Farm southeast of Moline. Two years later, McLain sold his operation to Mrs. Charles Deere Wiman, who donated it to Rock Island County. Eventually, this became Niabi Zoo.

By far the most dramatic effects on the lifestyle of the Quad Cities arose from a burgeoning population. Returning veterans, postponed marriages, and an influx of workers for the expanding industries stretched the seams of many local institutions and services, especially schools and churches. The same baby boom that hit the rest of the United States

Courtesy, Putnam Museum.

THE PLAYCRAFTERS, A LOCAL THEATRE GROUP, MOVED INTO THEIR PERMANENT HOME IN 1959. THE RESTORED BARN THEATRE IN MOLINE IS SHOWN HERE PRIOR TO ITS RENOVATION.

Photo by, P. Samuel Whitehead.

Courtesy, Davenport Public Library.

ABOVE LEFT *MOLINE COMMUNITY COLLEGE WAS THE FIRST DISTRICT COMMUNITY COLLEGE IN ILLINOIS WHEN IT WAS ESTABLISHED IN 1961. THE SCHOOL WAS LATER RENAMED BLACK HAWK COLLEGE. SCHOOLS LIKE BLACK HAWK COLLEGE OFFERED COURSES FOR STUDENTS PREPARING TO GO ON TO FOUR-YEAR COLLEGES AND ALSO PRACTICAL TRAINING JOBS IN SKILLED TRADES AND IN THE PUBLIC SERVICE SECTOR.*

LEFT *THE GROWING POPULATIONS AND EXPANDING CITIES FORCED NEW SCHOOLS TO BE BUILT FOR THESE BABY BOOMER CHILDREN. A NEW BETTENDORF HIGH SCHOOL OPENED ON 23RD STREET IN 1951. THIS HIGH SCHOOL BUILDING NOW HOUSES THE MISSISSIPPI BEND AREA EDUCATION AGENCY.*

created a critical housing shortage in the Quad Cities.

Among the first schools to face overcrowding were the three local colleges. As with other colleges and universities in the United States, Augustana and St. Ambrose were flooded with veterans making use of the G. I. Bill. Within three years, both had tripled their size. Augustana registered 1,130 students in 1946, and 1,803 in 1947. By 1948, St. Ambrose had an enrollment of 1,256, and a student body that was 85% veterans. Even the women's college, Marycrest, rose to 500 students in 1947 and was forced to build a new dormitory.

While the three liberal arts colleges adapted their curricula to accommodate the global and inter-connected post-war world, adding new courses in political science, geography, and Russian, they could not satisfy the needs of many veterans and others who sought more practical training for jobs in skilled trades or in the public service sector. The response to these needs was the community junior college. In 1946, the University of Illinois established a two year extension college in Moline. Moline Community College was

turned over to the Moline School District in 1948. It offered courses for students preparing to go on to four-year colleges, but it also offered an increasing number of courses for those training to become police officers, office personnel, draftsmen and other specific occupations. In 1961, when the State of Illinois established junior college districts, Moline Community College became the first district community college in Illinois and was renamed Black Hawk College.

Elementary and secondary schools, as well as other services, soon followed the growth of the colleges. Baby boomer children filled new grade schools in subdivision after subdivision. New paro-chial schools such as Rock Island Alleman High in 1949 and St Pius (later Jordan) in 1957 helped meet a classroom shortage. A new Bettendorf High School opened in 1951. By 1960 the boomers had come up through the system, and Davenport was forced to split its high school in two. West High opened that year on West Locust near the fringe of development, and the former Davenport High became Central. Hospital services expanded in 1960 with the opening of Davenport Osteopathic Hospital on Kimberly Road. Construction of all kinds boomed in the post-war years. Between 1945 and 1946, building tripled in Bettendorf, while Moline saw the beginning of 2,917 projects. A majority of area projects involved housing. The baby boom sent new young families scrambling for places to live and the cities scrambling for land on which to build the homes. Rock Island annexed ten additions in 1947 alone; Davenport annexed twenty additions in 1953. Davenport in several different years annexed land more than 100 times its original size in 1836, including 1957, when a 17-square-mile addition to the north and an 11-square-mile addition to the west made Davenport the second largest city in Iowa.

In contrast to the large 19th and early 20th century homes in the older neighborhoods ringing the downtowns, many of the new housing developments filled with much smaller homes suited to young families without much financial base looking for a place to start.

Some of these tract houses were small developments, such as the four-room Honeymoon Homes built in the 1400 block of South Michigan in Davenport, but several were larger than anything previously imagined. In the late 1940s, the Byrne-Moline Communities, Inc. began an addition of 510 two- and three-bedroom homes in southeast Moline. Molette, as it was called, was one of the largest single-housing projects in the Midwest. The homes were pre-fabricated on an assembly line on site in large Quonset hut shops. The project was originally planned as a complete community with shops, theaters, and offices, but these never materialized. Across the river, Molette was rivaled by an even larger development, Scott County's Ridgeview Park, with 654 houses. At its construction peak in 1953, one home was completed here every thirty minutes.

The housing boom continued strong throughout the 1950s. As late as 1959, more than a thousand homes a year were being built in the Quad Cities, often pushing the cities into competition for space. Davenport moved north and west out into farmland, Bettendorf went up and around Riverdale. In Illinois, Moline moved down into the Rock River valley and then across the river. Rock Island had more of a problem. Hemmed in a triangle by the Mississippi and the Rock rivers, and by the Moline border, Rock Island was forced in 1959 to jump the Rock River and annex a tract of land in southwest Rock Island County next to Milan.

This vast expansion of city space was made possible in great part by the automobile, now coming into its own. Just as the Civil War had called the

Government's attention to the importance of the river and the railroad, so World War II brought home the need for improved roads. Late in 1956, the Quad Cities learned of plans for a new four-lane interstate highway system designed to replace previous coast-to-coast roads such as the Lincoln Highway, rapidly becoming outmoded by the new pace of traffic. The plans called for Federal Interstate 6 (now I-80) to follow approximately the route of the old Chicago, Rock Island, and Pacific Railroad west from Chicago through the Quad Cities via a new bridge across the Mississippi between Port Byron and LeClaire. The north and east sections of FAI-6 around the cities was under construction by 1957.

In 1958, FAI-5 (now I-74) from Peoria to FAI-6 was added, insuring that the Quad Cities would remain, as it had been in a world of river and rail, an important transportation hub.

Air transport also became a regular part of the local economy after the war. In 1945, the Illinois Legislature established local airport authorities with taxing and bonding powers. Using this act, Rock Island County bought the Moline Airport in 1947, making it the official airport for the Quad Cities under the Quad City Airport Authority. An instrument landing system was installed in 1946, and air freight inaugurated. A new passenger terminal was dedicated in 1954. By the mid-1950s, more than 100,000 passengers annually were arriving at or leaving the Quad Cities by air. In Davenport, Cram Field was overrun by houses and businesses moving north, and was replaced in 1950 by a new airport at Mt. Joy.

Without as much fanfare as the airplane and the interstate, river and rail continued on as part of the local transportion story. Although the last electric train, the Rock Island Southern between the Quad Cities and Monmouth/Galesburg, went out of business in 1952, and the last commercial steam locomotive on the Burlington line left in 1954, there still remained four railroads and 40 passenger and freight trains a day out of Davenport. River traffic fared even better. Use of the river had slowed during the War, but returned quickly afterwards as the nine-foot channel lived up to expectations. A record number of towboats and barges were built in 1949, and throughout the 1950s, shipping set new records almost every year. The capacity of the modern tow boat and its barges dwarfed the once-impressive statistics from the golden age of steamboating. The 22 steamboats arriving at St. Paul in 1857 brought a total of 2,500 tons of freight. In 1947, the towboat *Alexander Mackenzie* took a cargo of 18,500 tons through the Quad Cities to St. Paul in a single trip.

The towboat Alexander Mackenzie took a cargo of 18,500 tons through the Quad Cities in a single trip in 1947. Less than one hundred years earlier, in 1857, twenty-two steamboats brought a total of only 2,500 tons of freight through the Quad Cities.

A single post-war barge can handle the equivalent of 35 to 45 railroad cars, with up to 17 barges in a single tow. Five million tons of freight passed through, to, or from the Quad Cities via river in 1950; by 1959 the figure had passed ten million tons.

Much of the money behind all the building, construction, expansion and increased goods and services came directly and indirectly from the large industries, especially the farm equipment businesses, which, in spite of recurrent labor troubles, enjoyed their best decade ever in the 1950s. The war years had built up a need for new machinery, and a new global economy opened a world-wide market for goods from the Quad Cities.

The growth of local economy began right after the war, but it was the Korean War in 1950 that marked the beginning of real prosperity. Military orders placed at local plants, and an increase in Arsenal employment of 40% in 1951 pushed the Quad Cities labor force to 95,000, 3,500 more than a year earlier. Case received a 4.5 million dollar order for airplane engine crankshafts, Eagle Signal obtained a million dollar order for Army teletype machines, and International Harvester in East Moline got an order for tank shoe treads.

Even without the military, local industries were doing well. Thirty-seven new corporations were formed in Scott County in 1952. Farmall had turned out its millionth tractor in 1951 (its 25th year), and was now producing 75,000 tractors a year–1,530 per week. Deere and Company did exceptionally well. Between 1946 and 1954, the company added many new products, including the first wire-tie baler, a self-propelled combine harvester, a self-propelled cotton picker, and a combine corn head. In 1955, William A. Hewitt became president of Deere and guided the company into the world market. Deere bought a

German tractor factory and land for a tractor plant in Mexico in 1956, and established an overseas division. That same year, Deere also began a separate industrial equipment division. Even running three shifts a day, it was difficult for local manufacturers to keep up with the demand.

By 1956, 318 manufacturing industries were located in the Quad Cities, including a new major equipment company, Caterpillar Tractor, which bought the Englehart Manufacturing Company and was planning a new plant east of Bettendorf.

During the 1950s, the Quad Cities downtowns shared in the prosperity. Retail merchants benefitted from the high employment and good wages, and local governments benefitted from good tax bases. Sears built a new $2,000,000 store in Davenport in 1950. Rock Island's Sunset Marina opened in 1956, along with a Younkers department store downtown, the same year *Life* magazine named Rock Island one of its "All American Cities."

For those who troubled to read them, however, there were disturbing signs that all was not well for the Quad Cities. The downtowns, especially Rock Island, were showing their age. The once grand hotels that had made rail passengers gape, were no longer first class, and were running into competition from new-fangled motels, designed for an automobile culture, with easy parking.

The car, in fact, was changing more than how far away a family could live. Parking space became a necessity for those who could no longer walk from home. In 1949, Davenport turned much of LeClaire Park along the riverfront into parking lots, and supplemented this with a three-level parking ramp at 5th and Brady in 1953. Similarly cramped for space, Rock Island was forced to use Spenser Square as the site for a new Post Office and Federal Building in 1954.

ABOVE RIGHT *THE FIRST DAIRY QUEEN STORE WAS OPENED IN MOLINE BY J.P. MCCULLOUGH IN 1941. DAIRY QUEEN WAS THE FIRST ICE CREAM STORE TO SERVE SOFT ICE CREAM. DAIRY QUEEN FRANCHISES WERE SPREADING ACROSS THE COUNTRY BY THE 1950S.*

RIGHT *SHOPPING STRIPS SUCH AS DUCK CREEK PLAZA WHICH OPENED IN 1960 AND THE VILLAGE SHOPPING CENTER WHICH OPENED IN 1956, WERE AN ADDITIONAL INCENTIVE FOR SHOPPERS TO LEAVE THE DOWNTOWNS.*

If the availability of cars after the war clogged the downtowns, those same cars made Quad Citians less interested in and less dependent on the downtown for almost every service. The post-war United States was characterized by a drive-in craze. Drive-in movies were followed by drive-in resaurants and drive-in bank facilities. Two drive-ins, one for sandwiches and another for ice cream, opened on 11th Street in Rock Island in 1947. The new chain supermarkets in the Quad Cities, A & P and National Tea opened stores with more parking lot than store.

At least two Quad Citians made important contributions to the drive-in culture. In 1941, J. F. McCullough opened an ice cream store in Moline, the first to serve soft ice cream. He named his store Dairy Queen. By the 1950s, Dairy Queen franchises were spreading across the country. Although company headquarters moved to Minneapolis, the machines to make the ice cream continued to be manufactured by the H. C. Duke Company in East Moline.

A more flambouyant entrepreneur than McCullough was Abraham L. Tunick, who had come to the Quad Cities in 1936 to work for his father-in-law, A. D. Harris, in the scrap metal business. In 1950, Tunick bought the bankrupt Dean Products Company and found himself with a large supply of fryers and cookers. In order to use this equipment, he decided to open a restaurant featuring "take-out" dinners, a new idea at the time. In 1952, Tunick opened the first Chicken Delight store on 18th Avenue in Rock Island. An immediate hit, Chicken Delight eventually became a franchise with 750 stores. His slogan, "Don't cook tonight, call Chicken Delight" became famous nationwide. No wonder then, that in the spring of 1958, when a strange building with two large golden arches appeared for the first time in Iowa on Brady Street Hill near Duck Creek, it attracted somewhat less attention than it might have.

No small-time entrepreneur, Al Tunick experimented with delivering his chicken dinners to area farms via small parachutes tossed from low flying delivery planes. At the height of Chicken Delight's success, Tunick sold out to Continental Foods and opened Franchise Growth to aid would-be entrepreneurs obtain franchises. He then went on to develop Karmelkorn Shops just as the mall craze was beginning, and sold out to Dairy Queen when the fun of developing was gone.

Throughout the 1950s, the drive-in stores continued to expand, along with other businesses that grew up along most of the major thoroughfares in the Quad Cities, all dependent on drawing customers in cars. Unlike the older neighborhood shopping districts such as Moline's Uptown and Rock Island's Hilltop, these new businesses depended on attracting customers from the entire Quad Cities and away from the downtowns. The high-volume supermarkets which anchored many of these developments needed customers who loaded a week's worth of groceries into a car rather than nearby families who walked home from the corner store with a few items for dinner.

By the mid-1950s, a natural extension of this change in shopping habits appeared. In the spring of 1956, the Village Shopping Center, with 29 stores, opened on West Kimberly followed by Duck Creek Shopping Center in 1960. These retail complexes offered a variety of stores from restaurants to clothing and hardware in one convenient location with plenty of parking.

Amid the prosperity and growing population of the post-war years in the Quad Cities, however, the downtowns were not yet frightened by the new developments. There were enough customers to go around. By 1960 Davenport had a population of 89,000, Rock Island, 52,000, Moline, 43,000, and East Moline, 17,000. A few businesses were pinched. Small neighborhood theaters were feeling the effects of television, and the smaller, local grocery stores, especially the mom-and-pop operations, were finding it difficult to keep up with the expectations of customers who had experienced a supermarket. But the mainline stores were doing well. Petersen's and Parker's in Davenport, McCabes and Younkers in Rock Island, and the New York Store in Moline continued to draw customers. Workers from other areas of the country continued to migrate to the Quad Cities, taking what temporary jobs they could find until the dream job opened up at Deere, Harvester, Case, or Alcoa.

CHAPTER SIX:

Weathering the Storms 1960-1980

IF SMOKESTACKS AND STORAGE TANKS DOMINATED THE RIVER SKYLINE OF THE QUAD CITIES BY 1960, THE COMMUNITIES THEMSELVES WERE OASES OF GREEN. As in many other Midwestern communities, the American elm had become the street tree of choice. In older neighborhoods, and along thoroughfares such as Rock Island's 7th Avenue, 80-foot high elms lined the steets, often arching overhead to meet and form green tunnels. Moline, the "City of Elms," was especially proud that an elm from the front yard of one of its residents, Henry Kuehl, had provided Luther Burbank with the seeds of an important commercial variety, *Ulmus americana Moline.*

By 1959, however, the first signs of Dutch elm disease appeared in a number of Quad Cities elms. Discovered in Cleveland, Ohio, in 1930, the disease had inexorably spread across the country. In spite of heroic efforts to treat the disease, the elms fell, singly at first and then block by block, so that by 1970, the three elder cities lay denuded of much of their green shade.

Dutch elm disease was the first of a series of storm fronts–natural, economic, and social–which crossed the United States in the 1960s and 70s and touched the Quad Cities in their sweep, bringing, as storms do, both refreshment and destruction.

At first, the Quad Cities in 1960 seemed impervious to all outside storms. The economic barometers pointed to continuing prosperity. Between 1960 and 1965, employment rose by 17%, the local payroll by 36%, retail sales by 51%, and housing starts by 61%. Employment in Scott and Rock Island counties reached a record 121,850 in 1964 and rose to 146,415 in 1966, with more local jobs available than workers to fill them.

For the farm equipment business, times were especially good. Caterpillar added new land for expansion in Bettendorf. Deere and Company, with increased international sales and a new consumer products divison took over first place in the industry in 1963. In 1966, Deere sales exceeded a billion dollars for the first time.

Under the glow of this prosperity, the Quad Cities continued to grow in both size and services. Silvis, East Moline, and Milan all annexed large sections of land, as did Bettendorf and Davenport. In 1960 a second span of the Iowa-Illinois Memorial Bridge opened between Moline and Bettendorf. It became the crossing point for I-74 in 1975 when that interstate was opened through Moline. Completion of the I-80 bridge between LeClaire and Rapid City in 1966 opened Interstate 80 from Chicago to Des Moines. By 1973, the I-280 bridge west of the Quad Cities completed the local interstate system. Ozark Airlines added the first jet service in the Quad Cities in l966.

Prosperity was also reflected in the amount and quality of new construction: a Sheraton-Rock Island

THE SECOND SPAN OF THE IOWA-ILLINOIS MEMORIAL BRIDGE ACROSS THE MISSISSIPPI BETWEEN MOLINE AND BETTENDORF WAS COMPLETED IN 1960. THIS BRIDGE BECAME THE CROSSING POINT FOR INTERSTATE 74 WHEN THAT INTERSTATE OPENED THROUGH MOLINE IN 1975.

Courtesy, Putnam Museum.

Courtesy, Putnam Museum.

Courtesy, Davenport Public Library.

hotel in 1966, and a new waterfront headquarters for Modern Woodmen in 1967. In 1964, Deere and Company moved into a stunning new administrative center designed by Eero Saarinen on 1,000 acres of carefully manicured wooded hills southeast of downtown Moline. Davenport in 1968 moved its public library into a new building designed by Edward Durrell Stone, architect for the Kennedy Center in Washington, D. C. Iowa-Illinois Gas and Electric Company began to draw power from the area's first nuclear generating station at Cordova, Illinois, in 1972.

Services grew as well. Illini Hospital opened in East Moline in 1968, while Franciscan Hospital in Rock Island in 1972 replaced the old St. Anthony's Hospital, which was turned into a continuing care center. As happened elsewhere in the country, the local college population more than doubled in the 1960s, sending local colleges into an expansion of

their services. Black Hawk added a second campus in Kewanee, Illinois, in 1967. Prospective students found their choices expanded by two new junior colleges. Palmer College of Chiropractic founded Palmer Junior College in 1965 to provide undergraduate work in the arts and sciences for area students as well as those interested in preparing to attend Palmer. That same year, the State of Iowa established the Eastern Iowa Community College District comprising junior colleges in Clinton and Muscatine, along with Scott Community College, whose vocational programs had previously been run out of the vocational departments of Scott County high schools and which now built its own campus in Riverdale. In 1979, Palmer Junior College merged with Scott to add an arts and sciences component to the vocational training. Expanded graduate opportunities also came to the Quad Cities in 1969 when a consortium of nine Iowa and Illinois state universi-

Courtesy, Deere and Company.

RIGHT *DAVENPORT RAZED ITS OLD CARNEGIE LIBRARY AND BUILT A NEW FACILITY IN 1968. THE NEW LIBRARY WAS DESIGNED BY EDWARD DURRELL STONE, ARCHITECT FOR THE KENNEDY CENTER IN WASHINGTON, D.C.*

LOWER RIGHT *PALMER COLLEGE OF CHIROPRACTIC FOUNDED PALMER JUNIOR COLLEGE IN 1965 TO PROVIDE UNDER-GRADUATE WORK IN THE ARTS AND SCIENCES FOR AREA STUDENTS AS WELL AS THOSE INTERESTED IN PREPARING TO ATTEND PALMER.*

LOWER LEFT *THE NEW NATIONAL HEAD-QUARTERS FOR MODERN WOODMEN OF AMERICA WAS A FIVE-STORY GLASS AND GRANITE BUILDING CONSTRUCTED ALONG THE WATERFRONT IN ROCK ISLAND IN 1967.*

Photo by P. Samuel Whitehead.

Courtesy, The Dispatch/The Rock Island Argus.

Courtesy, Davenport Public Library.

ties and private colleges began operation of the Quad Cities Graduate Studies Center to offer a wide range of courses in business, education, and selected fields.

Prosperity also brought new cultural opportunities to the Quad Cities. The Putnam Museum, in 1963, and the Davenport Museum of Art, in 1966, moved into spacious new quarters on top of the bluff just west of Marycrest College. In 1965, the opening of Scott County Park north of Davenport gave Iowa its first county park. An active Quad City writing community led David Collins, Moline high school teacher and children's author, to organize the Mississippi Valley Writer's Conference in the summer of 1973.

Sports opportunities expanded as well in the 60s and 70s. In 1960, a group called the Quad-City Baseball Fan Association leased the Davenport Municipal Stadium, obtained a Class A charter, and brought in the Braves for the 60-61 season. For the next seventeen years the Los Angeles Angels A team

played at the stadium; the Chicago Cubs A team played there from 1979 until 1985, when the Angels returned. In 1961, Douglas Park in Rock Island became the home of the World Softball Tournament until 1970.

Ball games were not the only choice. In 1971, the Quad Cities hosted its first Quad-Cities Open golf tournament at the Crow Valley Country Club. Since 1985, it has been the Quad Cities Hardees Golf Classic. Harness racing came to the Quad Cities in 1973 with the completion of the East Moline Downs.

In this fair economic weather of the 1960s, few Quad Citians bothered to read the subtle signs of approaching storm fronts. One of the signs of trouble lay close to home, made more visible by the loss of the elm trees. The older Quad Cities neighborhoods now lay naked and exposed. Some of the

Courtesy, Putnam Museum.

Courtesy, The Dispatch/The Rock Island Argus.

grandest of the old 19th century homes could no longer hide the fact that they were deteriorating. Many had been carelessly broken up into small apartment units, their ornamental work fallen off or removed, or covered by cheap asbestos or asphalt siding. They had ceased being neighborhoods, and were now simply bedrooms for a transient population. In the west ends of Davenport and Rock Island, rows of single family homes lay in equal disrepair amid unkempt yards filled with rusting and abandoned cars.

Although all the Quad Cities showed signs of urban blight, decay was most visible in Rock Island.

While Davenport and Moline had both diversified their economic base, Rock Island had remained dependent on its reputation as a retail center. By the mid-1960s, however, Rock Island retailing was in decline. In the early 1950s, the downtown area bounded by 16th and 19th Streets and by Third Avenue had contained more than 260 food stores, drug stores, restaurants, and shops. By 1967, only 150 remained. Of the 90 general merchandise stores in Rock Island in 1954, 30 had disappeared by 1967.

In addition, as a result of the rapid rise and fall of employment at the Arsenal during World War II,

Courtesy, Putnam Museum.

THE CATHOLIC INTERRACIAL COUNCIL WAS JUST ONE OF MANY GRASS ROOTS ORGANIZATIONS IN THE QUAD CITIES WHO WERE CONCERNED FOR CIVIL RIGHTS. ONE OF THEIR MAIN ISSUES WAS TO PASS OPEN HOUSING LAWS IN THE QUAD CITIES.

the west end of Rock Island had become a ghetto of unemployed and underemployed workers and their families. Many of these were blacks who were let go after the war, and who found themselves frustrated by both unions and industries in their attempts to find steady work.

It was natural, therefore, that the early attempts at urban renewal in the Quad Cities should be made in Rock Island's west end. The first of these was the 1960 Garnsey Square Urban Renewal Project. Using Federal financing under Title 1 of the Housing Act, the project sought to clear 165 parcels of land to make way for new businesses and new jobs. Delays pushed the starting date to 1963, and when the project books closed in 1966, little had been accomplished. The new industries—primarily warehouses, truck terminals and parking lots—added few jobs.

Rock Island then began a more ambitious project as part of President Johnson's War on Poverty. In 1966, Congress passed the Model Cities Act to improve the social, physical, and economic conditions in 150 American cities. In 1968, Rock Island became one of two cities (out of 163 applications that year) to be granted funds. Following a two-year planning period, using a number of local citizens, private and government agencies, and paid consultants, Rock Island began to construct a network of services in the west end, including the Alpha Adult Learning Center in 1971, and the Rainbow Child Development Center at Apollo Rocket Park the following year. HUD granted the Rock Island project an additional three million dollars in 1971, which was used to set up an extensive Head Start program, a neighborhood health clinic, a legal aid bureau, and the Youth Guidance Council. In 1974, ground was broken for the Martin Luther King Community Center at 7th Avenue and 9th Street.

Although the Model Cities program achieved modest success, the problems of poverty and urban blight proved more intractable than planners realized, and the project fell short of its goal.

As elsewhere in the country, efforts to improve the conditions in the inner Quad Cities inevitably came to involve civil rights. The Civil Rights Act of 1964, ordering schools to desegregate, outlawing segregation in all public facilities, and forbidding unions and industries alike from discriminating on the basis of sex, race, religion, or country of origin, added teeth to the long efforts of local minority groups to alleviate discrimination in housing and jobs. In the early 60s in the Quad Cities, many jobs were unavailable to blacks and hispanics, and many neighborhoods were unofficially off limits as far as housing was concerned.

Concerns for both civil rights and poverty led to the organization of several grass roots groups in Davenport and Rock Island. Attempts by groups such as the Davenport and Rock Island County Interracial Councils to pass open housing laws in the Quad Cities led several members, including Father Jack Real, assistant pastor at Sacred Heart in Rock Island, to organize Project NOW (Neighborhood Outreach Work) in 1968 in order to address the whole area of individual and civil needs. Until 1971, when it began to receive Federal and State funding, Project NOW operated with private donations and the support of a wide range of local volunteers. The current director of Project NOW, Vince Thomas, was an exchange student from Bombay, India, when

Courtesy, The Dispatch/The Rock Island Argus.

Courtesy, The Dispatch/ The Rock Island Argus.

he arrived in the Quad Cities in the late 1950s to work as a reporter at several local newspapers. His reportorial duties in the mid-60s drew him into the civil rights movement, where he became visible in many of the confrontations and marches, and in 1973, to the directorship of Project NOW.

Another citizen's organization still flourishing was born in 1976 when the Reverend Kenneth Kuehnning, pastor of the Church of Peace in Rock Island, formed the Community Caring Conference to residents in urban renewal areas to set up renters' action groups, crime watches, and other self-help programs.

The opening up of housing and jobs to minorities in the Quad Cities was not without confrontation–there were sit-ins and marches and arrests–but the slow movement toward civil rights here was more peaceful than in many similar industrial cities. This was due in part to the relatively small percentage of minorities in the Quad Cities–some 7%, to the support for rights from the white community, including many college students, and to many local industries such as Deere who voluntarily adopted affirmative action programs. But the peace was due in even greater part to the leadership in the black community itself which counseled moderation. One of the most influential of these leaders was the Reverend William Grimes, pastor of the Second Baptist Church of Rock Island, who came to the Quad Cities in the 1930s, and who had long been an advocate of achieving civil rights by example rather than confrontation. Although there were occasional rumors of Black Panther meetings in the Quad Cities, it was the more moderate groups such as the NAACP and Martin Luther King, Jr.'s Southern Christian Leadership Conference that served

as a pattern for the local black community. King's assassination on April 4, 1968, resulted in some violence, quickly put down by members of the black community.

Civil rights inched forward. In 1969, James Davis became the first black elected to the Rock Island City Council, serving until April of 1979, when he became the first black mayor in the Quad Cities.

Viet Nam was another storm that proved troubling for the Quad Cities. The increase in the draft quota in 1964 and the first sustained bombing of North Viet Nam in 1965 forced Quad Citians, as elsewhere, to take sides. In July of 1967, a steering committee of eight under Father Jack Smith of St. Ambrose College formed the Quad-Citians for Peace, which began a series of vigils for peace. In September, the group opened a draft counselling service for those facing the draft. That same fall, two members, Chuck and Judy Quilty, opened Omega House at 3826 7th Avenue in Rock Island, the first of a series of Catholic Worker Houses in the Quad Cities dedicated to pacifism and service to the poor.

The peaceniks met with immediate opposition. When the group requested permission from the Moline City Council to hold a silent vigil for peace at a local memorial in 1967, a vocal minority of council members descried the vigil as unpatriotic, a view shared by many Quad Citians, and by a tradition which went back at least to the strong support of the Civil War by Davenport's German immigrants. From these feelings came a war memorial in Silvis. Second Street in Silvis was a 200-yard-long unpaved road in the heart of a Mexican-American community. A

Courtesy, The Dispatch/The Rock Island Argus.

Courtesy, The Dispatch/The Rock Island Argus.

Courtesy, The Dispatch/The Rock Island Argus.

UPPER LEFT *FATHER JACK SMITH, OF ST. AMBROSE UNIVERSITY, LED A GROUP KNOWN AS THE QUAD-CITIANS FOR PEACE IN JULY OF 1967. THIS GROUP BEGAN A SERIES OF VIGILS FOR PEACE TO END THE VIETNAM WAR.*

LOWER LEFT *REVEREND WILLIAM GRIMES WAS A STRONG LEADER IN THE BLACK COMMUNITY DURING THE CIVIL RIGHTS MOVEMENT OF THE 1960S. HE WAS AN ADVOCATE OF ACHIEVING CIVIL RIGHTS BY EXAMPLE RATHER THAN VIOLENCE. GRIMES PLAYED A LARGE ROLE IN KEEPING THE SLOW MOVEMENT TOWARD CIVIL RIGHTS A PEACEFUL ONE IN THE QUAD CITIES.*

LEFT *JAMES DAVIS BECAME THE FIRST BLACK MAYOR IN THE QUAD CITIES WHEN HE WAS ELECTED MAYOR OF ROCK ISLAND IN 1979. BEFORE THIS, HE SERVED FOR TEN YEARS ON THE ROCK ISLAND CITY COUNCIL WHERE IN 1969 HE WAS THE FIRST BLACK ELECTED.*

record 57 men from this one block had served in World War II and in Korea. Of these, eight men from seven different families had died in action, including two of four Sandoval brothers who had been drafted. Another 27 men from this block would serve in Viet Nam. As the war in Viet Nam escalated, Silvis alderman Joe Terronez proposed renaming this street as a memorial to those who had served and died in America's wars. On Memorial Day, 1971, Silvis renamed this dirt road Hero Street (it was finally paved in 1975).

It was the protest against the war, however, that made the most headlines. In October of 1969, after the introduction of the draft lottery, the Quad-Citians for Peace held the first of many Viet Nam Moratoriums. The Arsenal brought in 150 combat troops to keep order on the island as nearly 1,500 college students and local residents marched by candlelight on both sides of the river to a meeting at LeClaire Park, where they read the names of soldiers killed in the war. That Christmas Eve, the peace group committed its first act of civil disobedience, as

15 people celebrated a mass for peace on the grounds of old Fort Armstrong, an area the Arsenal had declared off-limits. Resistance escalated the following spring following the United States' intervention in Cambodia. Demonstrators in front of the Rock Island Federal Building handed the IRS a list of 130 names of those who would no longer pay the federal "war" excise tax on telephone bills. On April 15, five protesters turned in their draft cards at the Federal Building as Federal marshalls watched. Protests continued to escalate, spurred on by events such as the shootings at Kent State in May of 1970, until 1973, when the last American troops left Viet Nam.

By then, a new rights movement was underway in the Quad Cities. On August 26, 1970, the 50th anniversary of the women's right to vote, a teach-in on women's rights organized by Linda Allen and Judy Quilty and featuring two members of the St. Ambrose faculty, Sisters Ritamary Bradley and Annette Walters, led to an organization called WE (Women for Equality), which, in 1971 affiliated with the National Organization of Women. The Quad Cities chapter became the second NOW chapter in Illinois. Among NOWs first actions was an attempt to stop local

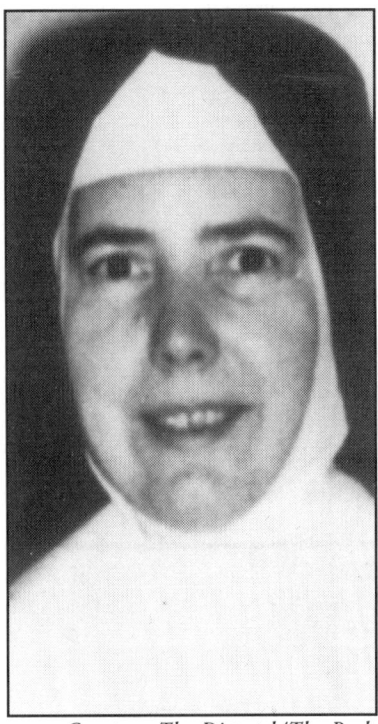

UPPER LEFT *JUDY QUILTY HELPED ORGANIZE A TEACH-IN ON WOMEN'S RIGHTS IN 1970 ON THE 50TH ANNIVERSARY OF THE WOMEN'S RIGHT TO VOTE. THIS TEACH-IN SPURRED THE WOMEN'S RIGHTS MOVEMENT IN THE QUAD CITIES.*

LOWER LEFT *HENRY HOOK WAS EDITOR OF THE DAVENPORT TIMES-DEMOCRAT WHEN THE QUAD CITIES CHAPTER OF THE NATIONAL ORGANIZATION OF WOMEN WANTED LOCAL NEWSPAPERS TO STOP SEPARATING WANT ADS INTO MALE AND FEMALE LISTINGS. HOOK DISAGREED AND SAID, "LADIES, I COULDN'T SLEEP AT NIGHT IF I THOUGHT SOME POOR WOMAN WAS WORKING IN A DIRTY JOB SHE READ ABOUT IN MY PAPER."*

CENTER TOP AND RIGHT *SISTERS RITAMARY BRADLEY AND ANNETTE WALTERS, TWO MEMBERS OF THE ST.*

AMBROSE UNIVERSITY FACULTY, HELPED TO FORM AN ORGANIZATION CALLED WE (WOMEN FOR EQUALITY). IN 1971, WE AFFILIATED WITH THE NATIONAL ORGANIZATION OF WOMEN.

LOWER RIGHT *OPPOSITION TO THE WAR IN VIETNAM CONTINUED TO ESCALATE IN REACTION TO EVENTS LIKE THE U.S. INVASION OF CAMBODIA AND THE SHOOTINGS AT KENT STATE IN MAY OF 1970. THIS PROTEST AT THE FEDERAL BUILDING IN DAVENPORT OCCURRED A FEW DAYS AFTER THE KENT STATE INCIDENT.*

Courtesy, Quad-City Times.

newspapers from separating want ads into male and female listings. *The Argus* agreed to change, but Henry Hook, editor of the *Davenport Times-Democrat,* refused, saying, "Ladies, I couldn't sleep at night if I thought some poor woman was working in a dirty job she read about in my paper." There were also positive signs. In 1971, Kathryn Kirschbaum became the first Quad Cities woman mayor when she was elected to the first of two terms in Davenport. That same year, Betty Denkhoff became the first woman corporate officer in the 134-year history of Deere and Company.

While these national storms of change were sweeping the Quad Cities in their passage across the country, more local storms were buffeting the cities themselves. It was clear that the downtowns of the three older cities were in trouble, plagued by decaying buildings and new shopping habits.

Attention to the problems of the downtowns would have come in any case, but it arrived dramatically in the spring of 1965 via the Mississippi River. The fall of 1964 and spring of 1965 had been especially wet seasons in the Upper Mississippi Valley, and by late March it became clear that there would be a major

flood. Floods were not a new experience for the Quad Cities. Wet decades in the 1820s, 1840s, 1880s, and the 1940s had each produced serious floods. The third worst local flood on record (exceeded only by floods in 1828 and 1851), had occurred in 1951, when 2,000 Quad Citians were forced out of homes and the river remained above flood stage for 22 days.

As the crest of the flood moved down the river in April of 1965, breaking all records along the way, Quad Citians braced for a predicted crest of 19.5 feet, 4.5 feet above flood stage. The Rock Island District Corps of Engineers supervised preparations to contain the flood, strengthening existing levees and constructing new ones with sandbags. A number of individual businesses and homeowners began to do their own sandbagging. The Mississippi went over flood stage in the Quad Cities on April 15 and continued to rise to a crest of 22.48 feet on April 28, far above estimates, threatening industries, downtowns, and city services.

The Mississippi remained above flood stage in the Quad Cities until May 12. The gradual upward slope of downtown Davenport kept the water from going much beyond Second Avenue, but Rock Island, on low ground, was especially vulnerable. Had it not been for round-the-clock volunteer help from the Red Cross, the National Guard, the Mennonite Disaster Service, and local high school and college students whose classes were suspended so they could fill and place sandbags, the damage to Rock Island businesses would have been much worse.

The flood of 1965 left the Quad Cities with an unpleasant decision: to build a flood wall against future floods and so intrude on the view of the river, or to keep access to the river open, and so invite damage from future floods. Rock Island eventually elected to build a crushed rock levee, hiding much of the river. Begun in 1970, the Rock Island levee was completed by 1973 in time to protect the city from another flood that year, fifth highest on record. After much protracted debate, and damage from the 1973 flood, Davenport eventually decided in 1984 against

THE SPRING FLOOD OF 1965 WAS THE WORST FLOOD ON RECORD IN THE QUAD CITIES. THE MISSISSIPPI RIVER CRESTED AT MORE THAN SEVEN FEET OVER FLOOD STAGE AND REMAINED ABOVE THE FLOOD STAGE FOR ALMOST A MONTH. THIS VIEW SHOWS THE EFFECT OF THE FLOOD ON JOHN O'DONNELL STADIUM IN DAVENPORT.

Courtesy, Davenport Public Library.

Courtesy, Davenport Public Library.

replaced by more permanent and more up-scale discount stores that came to stay: Target, K-Mart, and Venture. These stores, with name brand goods, provided serious competition for the downtown department stores.

blocking its view of the Mississippi..

Even as the floods called attention to the vulnerability of the downtowns, however, those downtowns were under threat from another source. Newer and larger businesses were locating out of the downtowns at strip shopping centers along major thoroughfares with easy access and better parking. Auto dealerships and supermarkets were among the first to opt for the open spaces.

Shopping patterns changed as well. Just as the supermarket chains had made life difficult for small local groceries, so other retailers began copying the supermarket way of doing things. In the early 1960s, discount houses appeared in the Quad Cities. The first of these, Spartan, Arlans, and Thrifttown, followed by Giant, Turnstyle, and Zayres, were no-frills stores selling inexpensive brands. The early discount stores did not last more than a few years,

By the end of the 1960s, several major department stores had already closed their doors. These included Moline's Block and Kuhl, the New York Stores in both Rock Island (1962) and Moline (1966), Hill's Department Store in Davenport (1963) and Younker's in Rock Island (1966).

Gradually, shoppers moved out of the downtowns to shopping strips such as Duck Creek and the Village Shopping Center, and to many newer ones such as Spring Village, North Gate, and Old Town which followed. This movement culminated in the early 1970s in the enclosed shopping mall. Northpark Mall, a project of the General Growth Corporation of Des Moines, opened in July 11, 1973, with 160 shops on 117 acres at Kimberly Road and Brady Street. A slightly smaller version, Southpark Mall, opened south of downtown Moline close to the Rock River in 1974. The enclosed mall, with its many stores, with a main avenue and side streets, became virtually another, newer downtown without parking problems, safe from the weather, and with more convenient hours than the old downtowns.

The malls drew customers from the downtowns, but they drew businesses, too. The many small specialty shops in the malls depended for their success on the drawing power of large anchor department stores. Northpark opened with Wards, Pennys, and Younkers, while Southpark anchors were Peterson's, Wards, and Younkers. Except for

Photo by, P. Samuel Whitehead.

THE ROCK ISLAND YMCA CLOSED ITS
DOWNTOWN BUILDING ON 20TH STREET IN
1977 AND OPENED A NEW CENTER FURTHER
SOUTH ON 24TH STREET NEAR BLACKHAWK
ROAD THE SAME YEAR.

Petersen's, the downtown versions of these stores
closed as part of their move to the mall. Competition
from the malls and shopping strips also closed other
major downtown department stores in the 1970s.
Carson, Pirie, Scott left Moline in 1974 while Parker's
closed in Davenport that same year. By 1980, only two
old historic department stores remained: Petersen's in
Davenport and McCabe's in Rock Island.

Other businesses and many of the cities' service
establishments also left the downtowns in the 1970s.
The last of the Weyerhaeuser lumber businesses, Rock
Island Lumber, Moline Building Center, and the East
Moline Lumber Store, all closed in 1970. Lefstein's
Clothing Store in Rock Island closed in 1971. Rock
Island's attempt to restore its downtown with the
Great River Plaza project in 1976 created construction
delays that caused Mosenfelder's, a 100-year-old
clothing store, to go under. The last of the grand
movie palaces in downtown Davenport, the Orpheum,
showed its last movie in September of 1973, while the
Fort Theater in Rock Island was reduced to showing
porno films, victims of the opening of a large movie
complex, Cinemas I and II in 1968 and Cinema III in
1970 in Milan. The Rock Island YMCA closed its
downtown center in 1977 and opened a new Y at 24th
Street near Black Hawk Road. The Moline YMCA
followed suit.

Fortunately for the local economy, industries
remained strong during this period. Case in Rock
Island had closed in 1961, but it reopened in 1965 to
produce hydraulic cylinders. The 40 foundries which
had once supplied the heavy demands of local
industries were meeting competition from foreign
foundries and were closing one by one, among them
the Farmall Plant Foundry which poured its last iron
on December 8, 1967. But most other businesses
seemed strong. Deere sales had reached 5.5 billion by
1980.

It was the filing for bankruptcy of the Rock
Island Lines in 1975 that brought on the first tremors
of an economic storm. At first, the bankruptcy
seemed merely an annoyance. The Rock had survived
bankruptcies in 1915 as a result of overbuilding and in
1933 as a result of the Depression, and in each case
had survived and become stronger. By 1945, the Rock
was making a profit of 20 million a year.

The Rock even developed a new logo in 1975 and
a new blue, white, and black color scheme. But this
time it was not to be. A merger with the Union Pacific
Railroad fell through in 1974, the same year the Rock
Island station in Davenport was torn down. Local
passenger service on the Rock Island Lines ended in
1979. In 1979 a series of severe storms in the Midwest
dried up revenues, and in August a strike over retroac-
tive pay during the height of the harvest season
pushed the Rock over the edge. The following January
a federal judge ordered liquidation of lines. On April
1, 1980, the Rock Island Lines, long a symbol of the
Quad Cities, ceased to exist, putting the Silvis Shops
out of business and 7,000 employees out of work.

Toward the end of the 1970s, the market for
farm equipment began to soften. The arbitration of
the late 50s and early 60s gave way to rising employer
resistance to unions, resulting in a growing number of
bitter strikes. These reached a peak in 1979 with one
or more stikes going on constantly all year at more
than a dozen places, including Black Hawk College,
Ozark Airlines, Oscar Mayer, and by numerous crafts
such as bakery workers, painters, electricians, and

bricklayers.

Of all these strikes, the most critical were those at the farm equipment plants. Deere, Caterpillar, and International Harvester all had UAW contracts ending in 1979, and all three were struck. The strike at Deere lasted only 21 days, but the Caterpillar strike lasted for 80 days.

International Harvester ran into the most trouble. Under a new, cost-cutting CEO, Archie McCardell, International Harvester took an inflexible stand, resulting in a traumatic 173-day strike at the IH plants in the Quad Cities. The company lost 222 million dollars during the first three months of the strike and another 300 million during the first quarter of 1980. By the time the strike ended in mid-1980, a recession had stalled the heavy truck market, and IH sales plummeted.

By the end of the 1970s, then, good times seemed over for both the downtowns and for local business and industry. While the smaller communities had grown during the decade–Bettendorf by 23%, Milan by 29%, Silvis by 20%, and Andalusia by 30%–the big three either lost population, as in the case of Rock Island and Moline, or had barely remained even, as in the case of Davenport.

If the storms of the 60s and 70s shook the foundations of the Quad Cities, they did not destroy it, and they had at least one positive effect of bringing the separate cities into closer cooperation with each other. The problems of urban renewal, poverty, and especially the growing environmental concerns arising in areas such as landfills and the increasing multi-purpose and competing uses of the river for transportation, for industry, for recreation, for commercial fishing, and for drinking water forced the cities to take each other into consideration more than ever.

The increasing complexity of the problems and the interrelatedness of the Quad Cities led to the formation of the Bi-State Metropolitan Planning Commission in 1966, to coordinate planning among the cities and to increase buying power of the individual governmental units. A number of other businesses and services also merged into Quad Cities organizations during this period. In 1962, 78 industries and businesses on both sides of the Mississippi united to form the Iowa-Illinois Industrial Development Group to attract new companies. This became the Quad-City Development Group in 1967. Other cooperative efforts included the Quad City Builder's Association, the Quad-City Federation of Labor, and the Quad City Chamber of Commerce Presidents. In 1965, the Rock Island Community Chest and other similar groups in Moline, East Moline, and Silvis merged into the United Appeal of Rock Island County, and this, in 1971, became the United Way of Scott and Rock Island Counties. More than 100 congregations and 12 Catholic parishes organized in –as Churches United of Scott and Rock Island Counties. Many businesses followed suit. In 1975, the _Davenport Times-Democrat_ became the _Quad-City Times_. In 1981, Rock Island's First National Bank became the First National Bank of the Quad Cities. In 1972, Rand McNally began using the name "Quad Cities" on its road maps and atlases. These cooperative ventures helped the Quad Cities survive the storms of change in the 60s and 70s as they pointed the way to the future.

CHAPTER SEVEN:

Soaring Ahead

I N 1980, THE QUAD-CITY DEVELOPMENT GROUP
MOUNTED AN EXTENSIVE MEDIA CAMPAIGN INVITING
QUAD CITIANS TO "FLY WITH THE EAGLE." THE
"Quad Cities USA," claimed the jingle, was "Looking
Better Every Day."

The slogan was easy to believe. In spite of the
demise of the Rock Island Lines in April, business
appeared to be rebounding from the problems of the
late 70s. Deere and Company, employing some 15,000
workers in its five local plants, was remodeling and
growing. Caterpillar Tractor was in the midst of
quadrupling its plant at the north edge of Davenport.
International Harvester, having ended a 173-day
strike—longest in its history—broke ground for a
large computer-controlled warehouse at the Farmall
Plant in Rock Island.

Non-farm businesses were also doing well.
Employment had risen to 7,500 at an expanding
Arsenal, Alcoa was increasing capacity, Hormel moved
into a new modern meat processing plant, Martin-
Marietta was completing construction of a 90-million-
dollar cement plant at Buffalo, and Honda had opened
a 10-million-dollar parts warehouse in northwest
Davenport. Median family income reached $22,878 by
the end of 1980, putting the Quad Cities among the
top fifty markets in the United States.

The optimism of 1980 turned out to be prema-
ture. The hardening stances of both labor and
management reflected by the UAW strike at International Harvester were heightened by the Professional
Air Traffic Controllers strike in August of 1981.
Media coverage of this strike, in the Quad Cities as
elsewhere, helped turn public opinion into a growing
suspicion of all unions.

This confrontational mood came at the same
time that the farm equipment business was battered
by outside events. A government set-aside program
idled 80 million acres of farm land, reducing the need
for new machinery, and sending local manufacturers
into the 1982 recession in already weakened condi-
tion. By the end of the year, more than 35,000
workers in Quad Cities plants had been idled,
sending unemployment levels above 17%. Farm
equipment sales by 1984 dropped to one-third of
what they had been in 1979.

For the Quad Cities' claim to be the farm
equipment capital of the world, it was the beginning
of the end. The giant conglomerate, International
Harvester, weakened by the 1979 strike and the poor
farm economy of the early 1980s, fell apart. Following a string of layoffs and shutdowns beginning in
1981, IH sold its Ag Equipment Group to Tenneco,
already the parent company of J. I. Case, in 1985.
The last Big Red tractor rolled off the line at Farmall

THE POOR FARM ECONOMY OF THE EARLY
1980S CONTRIBUTED GREATLY TO THE
DOWNFALL OF INTERNATIONAL HAR-
VESTER. THE LAST BIG RED TRACTOR
ROLLED OFF THE LINE AT FARMALL ON
MAY 14, 1985, AND THE PLANT CLOSED
THE FOLLOWING YEAR.

Courtesy, Putnam Museum.

DURING THE 1980S, THE ENTIRE QUAD CITIES SAW SOME OF THEIR MOST ESTAB-LISHED BUSINESSES LEAVE. ONCE A FIXTURE OF AMERICAN MAIN STREETS, THE WOOLWORTH VARIETY STORES IN DAVENPORT AND ROCK ISLAND CLOSED IN 1988 AND 1989. THE MANAGER OF THE DAVENPORT WOOLWORTH'S IS SHOWN HERE LOCKING THE DOORS FOR THE LAST TIME.

Courtesy, Quad City Times.

on May 14, 1985, and the plant closed the following year. Caterpillar closed its remanufacturing plant in Bettendorf in 1986, and its 2.5 million square-foot Mt. Joy plant north of Davenport in 1987, the same year that Case announced the closing of its plants in Rock Island and Bettendorf. Deere cut back its production and workforce and survived in better shape than the others, but it underwent a six-month strike in the last half of 1986, surpassing the previous record strike in 1950, and it did not return to profit-ability until the late 1980s.

Meanwhile, the flight from the downtowns showed little signs of easing. In 1973, at the beginning of that flight, Greg Cusack, Iowa State Representative and former Davenport alderman, had warned his community that "if we are going to save Davenport, we are going to have to do it in 20 years or lose it." Four years later, a *Quad-City Times* editorial had pronounced Davenport "a sinking ship."

All three cities saw some of their most estab-lished businesses leave in the 1980s. Mosenfelder's, a 100-year-old clothing store in Rock Island, closed in 1982, followed by the disappearance of another landmark, McCabe's Department Store, in 1984. The Fort Armstrong Hotel in Rock Island and the LeClaire Hotel in Moline, unable to find buyers, closed within a month of each other in 1983. The closing of the downtown Petersen's Department Store in Davenport in 1986, according to a city planner, "signaled the end of significant retailing in Davenport." Once a fixture of most American main streets, the Woolworth variety stores in Davenport and Rock Island closed in 1988 and 1989. The movie

theater disappeared from the downtown Quad Cities with the closing of *The Capri* in Rock Island in 1989.

By the late 1980s, an evening walk in downtown Rock Island, Moline, or Davenport was a lonely, and sometimes frightening, excursion. Closed stores, boarded-up windows, and deteriorating buildings gave the appearance of a war zone—a comparison not inappropriate in some sections of the downtowns which had become hangouts for drug buyers and sellers, and for local versions of Chicago street gangs. Unavoidable signs of homelessness and poverty reminded Quad Citians that "looking better every day" depended on where one looked.

The feelings of helplessness were heightened during the 1980s by the loss of many local and family businesses to "outsiders." Forgetting that outsiders had always been a part of the local business economy (the Deeres, Weyerhaeusers and Bettendorfs had themselves all been outsiders), Quad Citians saw the takeovers as symbols of the powerlessness of the local economy up against national and global trends. Many local banks and savings and loan companies merged with large conglomerates in other cities. The Potter family sold its interest in the *Argus* to the Small Newspaper Group in 1986, and its radio station WHBF to an eastern corporation in 1987. Bituminous Casualty in Rock Island was taken over by Old Republic International in 1984. In 1986 Servus Rubber became a subsidiary of Norcross Companies of Louisville, Kentucky. The confidence of Quad Citians was stretched further in the summer of 1991 when V. O. Figge, the legendary president of Davenport Bank and Trust, whose conservative fiscal policies had rescued the bank in the Great Depres-sion and turned out profits every year since then, announced the sale of the bank to the Norwest Corporation.

Even nature seemed to have saved her most perverse moments for later. On June 16, 1990, between 5 to 9 inches of rain fell on the Iowa Quad Cities in a few hours. With so much of Davenport and Bettendorf in the Duck Creek drainage basin given over to new construction and paved parking lots, the rain rushed into Duck Creek itself, sending the water level 8 to 10 feet above normal. The current in Duck Creek reached 35 miles an hour, covered many of the bridges along the way, closing major roads, flooding some 400 homes, and collaps-ing many basements. Between 400 and 500 people were evacuated, many of whom had thought that

Left *Duck Creek flooded its banks twice within two weeks in June of 1990. The current in Duck Creek reached 35 miles an hour during the first flood and over 400 homes were flooded out. These Davenport residents used a canoe to save some of thier belongings.*

Lower Left *Ben Butterworth, a Moline park board member, convinced Deere and Company to donate its land between River Drive and the Mississippi to the city of Moline in the 1960s.*

Lower Right *The strip of land Deere and Company donated to the city of Moline near the Mississippi was turned into playgrounds, picnic areas, and a two-mile paved bike path. The area was named the Ben Butterworth Parkway.*

their homes on top of the bluffs were safe. Another 5 1/2 inches of rain on Friday, June 29, sent Duck Creek over its banks to again flood many of the same homes.

Many Quad Citians kept believing that the good old days would return. There were rumors of a resurrected McCabes, a Japanese car maker coming to the empty Farmall plant. It took some time for city planners to realize that these changes, like those taking place in similar American cities, were not reversable.

Neither, as it turned out, were those changes fatal. "Fly with the Eagle" hung on both as a jingle and as an attitude. It was picked up by other advertisers in other campaigns, indicative of an upbeat attitude among Quad Citians that belied the evidence. That attitude involved a determination to act, to move on.

One small group of Quad Citians believed that a return to the river was a good place to start. As early as 1974, the *Quad-City Times* called for such a rediscovery. "It it weren't for the river, Davenport wouldn't be here," an editorial of January 27 noted. Pointing out that the downtown riverfront had been turned into a parking lot in the 1950s, and that only 10 blocks of Davenport's 9.5-mile riverfront had public access, with not a single public boat launching

Courtesy, The Dispatch/The Rock Island Argus.

Courtesy, Putnam Museum.

ABOVE LEFT THE QUEEN OF HEARTS WAS ONE OF TWO EXCURSION BOATS THAT BEGAN OFFERING LUNCH, DINNER, AND EVENING CRUISES FROM THE QUAD CITIES IN 1984. THE OTHER BOAT WAS THE MISSISSIPPI QUEEN WHICH ALSO RAN DAY-LONG TRIPS TO DUBUQUE AND BACK.

ABOVE RIGHT THE PRINCESS WAS JUST ONE OF MANY EXCURSION BOATS THAT OPERATED ON THE MISSISSIPPI RIVER IN THE QUAD CITIES BEGINNING IN THE MID-1980S. THESE EXCURSION BOATS ATTRACTED BUSLOADS OF TOURISTS FROM ALL OVER THE UNITED STATES AND CONVINCED QUAD CITIANS THAT TOURISM COULD BE A LUCRATIVE BUSINESS FOR THAT AREA.

LEFT THE JULIA BELLE SWAIN, AN AUTHENTIC STEAM-DRIVEN STERN-WHEELER, BEGAN OFFERING OVERNIGHT EXCURSIONS FROM LECLAIRE UPRIVER TO GALENA, ILLINOIS, IN 1987. THE BOAT IS HERE NEAR COMPLETION IN 1971.

Courtesy, The Dispatch/ The Rock Island Argus.

ramp, the editorial suggested that Davenporters had turned their backs on the river and that "now it is time that we establish top priority to bringing its beauty back to us."

Moline had already caught the river spirit by 1970. In the 1960s, Ben Butterworth, a park board member, had convinced Deere & Company to donate its land between River Drive and the Mississippi to the city. Following his death in 1969, Moline began turning this strip into the Ben Butterworth Parkway, with playgrounds, picnic areas, and a two-mile paved path for biking and walking.

Over the next few years, environmental groups and others, aided by a new Corps of Engineers Visitor Center at Locks and Dam 15, called attention to the Mississippi. The Junior League of the Quad-Cities declared 1983 the Year of the River and hosted a major conference bringing together a variety of river users.

But it was, ironically, outsiders who really helped the Quad Cities rediscover its river. In the summer of

1982, a small launch, the *Belle of Princeton*, began offering river excursions upriver from the Quad Cities. In 1984 two excursion boats began offering lunch, dinner, and evening cruises from the Quad Cities themselves: Joe Schadler's *Queen of Hearts*, operating from the Oneida Street landing in Davenport, and Robert Kehl's *Mississippi Queen* from the Bettendorf waterfront just below the I-74 bridge. In addition, the *Mississippi Queen* ran day-long trips to Dubuque and back. Amid the skepticism of many Quad Citians, who wondered out loud and in print why tourists would want to come to Davenport, the tourists came by the busloads from across the country to spend a brief two hours on the Mississippi River.

The success of that first season led Schadler to add a smaller boat, the *Princess*, in 1985. In 1987, two additional boats, the *Twilight* and the *Julia Belle Swain*—an authentic steam-driven stern-wheeler—began offering overnight excursions from LeClaire upriver to Galena, Illinois.

Quad Citians who had considered the Mississippi little more than an obstacle in traveling between Iowa and Illinois now discovered that they were

THE QUAD CITIES SYMBOLIZED THE
RETURN TO THE MISSISSIPPI RIVER IN
1988 WHEN THREE ARCHES OF THE
CENTENNIAL BRIDGE WERE LIT UP. THIS
VIEW SHOWS ELECTRICIANS ON THE ARCHES
OF THE BRIDGE INSTALLING THE LIGHTS.

THE CITY OF DAVENPORT BOUGHT STE. GENEVIEVE, A DECOMMISIOINED CORPS OF ENGINEERS
DREDGE, IN 1985. THE STE. GENEVIEVE WAS LOCATED ALONG THE LECLAIRE PARK SEAWALL
AND SERVED AS A FLOATING MUSEUM AND CLASSROOM.

"joined by a river," as the Junior League's 1983 theme proclaimed. Following the tourists out onto the river, they rediscovered its beauty and its history. American bald eagles had been wintering in the vicinity of the open water below Locks and Dams 14 and 15 since the 1930s, little noticed except by bird watchers and environmentalists. Now hundreds of Quad Citians made winter pilgrimages to watch eagles.

Where possible, waterfront areas lost to parking lots and industrial developments were reclaimed for parks and overlooks. Rock Island and Davenport followed Moline in increasing public access to the river. By 1991, East Moline had connected its own 3.1-mile bike path along the river to the Ben Butterworth Parkway. In 1984, Davenport shelved its plans for a flood control project in favor of maintaining an unobstructed view of the river. A year later, the city bought a decommissioned Corps of Engineers dredge, the _Ste. Genevieve_ and installed it as a floating museum and classroom along the LeClaire Park seawall. One visible sign of this return to the river was the lighting of the three arches of the Centennial Bridge in 1988. The Quad Cities riverfront today is busy with river festivals and celebrations every week during the season.

The rediscovery of the majesty of the Mississippi helped to reawaken the Quad Cities to its own rich past. Early Quad Citians were fascinated with themselves—the first written history of the good old days appeared less than twenty years after Rock Island and Davenport were founded—but there had been no comprehensive histories since the early 20th century. Now, as the cities approached their 150th anniversaries in the 1980s, new histories appeared. Rock Island, Davenport, Moline, Milan, LeClaire, and Andalusia each published community histories. In addition, there were two general histories of the Quad Cities. The Village of East Davenport recovered its past in restoration rather than words. This historic sawmilling center had become a ghost town by 1970, leaving Boyler's Blacksmith Shop as the only open store. Encouraged by Karen Anderson and others, local residents and newcomers began restoring shops and homes that were among the oldest in the Quad Cities.

The Village of East Davenport today is a 160-acre, 60 block area of shops and homes that has become a model for subsequent restoration projects by such new groups as the Col. Davenport Historical Foundation (1981). In 1979, Davenport hired Marlys Svendsen as its first city historian; her efforts helped Davenport place more than 100 properties on the National Register of Historic Places.

Today, historic preservation projects, both private and public, are busy preserving much of the

Photo by P. Samuel Whitehead.

Photo by P. Samuel Whitehead.

Courtesy, Rock Island County Historical Society.

Courtesy, The Dispatch/The Rock Island Argus.

CENTER RIGHT *MARLYS SVENDSEN WAS HIRED BY THE CITY OF DAVENPORT IN 1979 AS THE FIRST CITY HISTORIAN. SHE WAS INSTRUMENTAL IN PLACING MORE THAN 100 DAVENPORT PROPERTIES ON THE NATIONAL REGISTER OF HISTORIC PLACES. HER BOOK, DAVENPORT: A PICTORIAL HISTORY ALSO HELPED TO PROMOTE THE SIGNIFICANCE OF DAVENPORT'S PAST.*

LOWER LEFT *THE CARMELITE MONASTERY WAS BUILT IN BETTENDORF FROM 1915-17. IT HOUSED CARMELITE NUNS WHOSE STRICT ORDER HAD RULES OF SILENCE AND FASTING. MANY YEARS LATER, THE FRANCISCAN BROTHERS TOOK OVER AND CALLED THE HOME ST. FRANCIS MONASTERY. RECENTLY, THE MONASTERY BECAME THE ABBEY HOTEL.*

Courtesy, Davenport Public Library.

UPPER LEFT *THE DEERE-WIMAN HOUSE WAS ANOTHER RECENT HISTORIC PRESERVATION PROJECT IN THE QUAD CITIES. THE MOLINE HOME IS NOW FULLY RESTORED AND IS OPEN TO THE PUBLIC.*

UPPER RIGHT *THE ROCK ISLAND COUNTRY HISTORICAL SOCIETY DEDICATED ITS NEW WING LATE IN 1992. THE NEW SPACE AND EXPANDED HOURS HELPED TO MAKE MATERIAL MORE READILY AVAILABLE TO THE PUBLIC.*

CENTER LEFT *THE VELIE MANSION WAS HOME TO WILLARD LAMB VELIE, THE GRANDSON OF JOHN DEERE, AND HIS FAMILY. VELIE AND HIS SON HELPED TO MAKE MOLINE A CENTER FOR AUTOMOBILE PRODUCTION IN THE EARLY 20TH CENTURY, UNTIL THE DEATH OF THE TWO MEN JUST MONTHS APART IN 1929.*

Photo by, P. Samuel Whitehead.

Photo by, P. Samuel Whitehead.

Photo by, P. Samuel Whitehead.

UPPER AND CENTER LEFT THE QUAD-CITY TIMES BEGAN CONSTRUCTION OF ITS NEW HEADQUARTERS IN DAVENPORT IN 1990. THE NEW BUILDING IS LOCATED BETWEEN 3RD AND 4TH STREETS AT RIVER DRIVE. WORKERS ARE SHOWN HERE POURING CEMENT FOR THE BUILDING'S FOUNDATION AND THE FINISHED PRODUCT IS ALSO SHOWN.

ABOVE RIGHT THE VALE APARTMENTS IN DAVENPORT WERE TORN DOWN IN EARLY 1993 AFTER A LONG LEGAL BATTLE BETWEEN THE OWNER AND THE CITY. THE VALE, WHICH WAS EARLIER KNOWN AS THE KIMBALL HOUSE, WAS ONCE HOME TO FORMER PRESIDENT RONALD REAGAN IN THE LATE 1930S.

Photo by, P. Samuel Whitehead.

Courtesy, The Dispatch/The Rock Island Argus.

Courtesy, The Dispatch/The Rock Island Argus.

ABOVE LEFT IN 1982, THE CITY OF DAVENPORT BEGAN WORK ON RIVER CENTER, A NINE MILLION DOLLAR CONVENTION AND ENTERTAINMENT COMPLEX ADJACENT TO THE RESTORED BLACK HAWK HOTEL, AND OPENED THE NEW STRUCTURE IN 1983.

ABOVE RIGHT AND CENTER THE ORPHEUM THEATER, AFTER FOUR YEARS OF RENOVATION, OPENED AS THE ADLER THEATER IN 1986. IT WAS NAMED FOR EMMANUEL P. ADLER AND HIS SON, PHILLIP D. ADLER. THE TWO MEN WERE FORMER PRESIDENTS OF LEE ENTERPRISES AND CIVIC LEADERS IN DAVENPORT.

Quad Cities' past. The Davenport House, the LeClaire mansion, Clifton Manor, the Deere-Wiman House, the Velie home, the Butterworth and Hauberg homes are all in process or fully restored, and most are in use. In Moline, Montgomery Elevator has remodeled and restored the old post office on Third Avenue into a company headquarters. Individual

Courtesy, H.G.C. Incorpororated.

Courtesy, The Dispatch/The Rock Island Argus.

UPPER RIGHT *CIRCA 21 DINNER THEATER OPENED IN THE REMODLED FORT THEATER BUILDING IN ROCK ISLAND IN 1978. IT SERVED AS A MODEL FOR OTHER RESTORATION PROJECTS AND HELPED ATTRACT SEVERAL NEW RESTAURANTS AND NIGHT SPOTS TO THE DOWNTOWN.*

CENTER *MOLINE BEGAN CONSTRUCTION OF SUPERBLOCK, A SEVEN-STORY OFFICE BUILDING, IN JANUARY 1991. THE PROJECT WAS COMPLETED IN MARCH 1992 AND THE NAME WAS CHANGED TO HERITAGE PLACE FOR ITS MAIN TENANT, HERITAGE NATIONAL HEALTHPLAN. THIS ARTIST'S SKETCHBOARD SHOWED HOW HERITAGE PLACE WOULD LOOK WHEN COMPLETED.*

RIGHT *DENNIS HITCHCOCK, A FORMER THEATER TEACHER AT AUGUSTANA COLLEGE, OPENED CIRCA 21 DINNER THEATER IN 1978. HITCHCOCK'S SUCCESSFUL BUSINESS VENTURE WAS JUST THE BEGINNING OF "THE DISTRICT," THE NAME GIVEN TO THE EASTERN SECTION OF DOWNTOWN ROCK ISLAND IN 1991.*

Courtesy, The Dispatch/The Rock Island Argus.

homeowners began moving into Rock Island's Broadway Historic District and restoring homes to their original designs, returning, home by home, a whole neighborhood to its former glory.

Several local museums developed exhibits to reflect this renewed interest in local history. The Hauberg Indian Museum in Black Hawk State Park made more authentic its exhibits of Sauk and Mesquakie cultures, while the Jonathan M. Browning Museum at the Arsenal, featuring guns and other military weapons, became the Rock Island Arsenal Museum in 1986 to emphasize local arsenal history. In 1985, the Putnam Museum in Davenport capped a

gradual move toward becoming a regional museum with the opening of a permanent "River, Prairie, and People" exhibit. Specialized groups such as the Center for Belgian Culture (1964) and the Swenson Swedish Immigration Center (1981) grew out of an interest in keeping the history of Quad Cities' ethnic groups alive.

Along with the rediscovery of the river and the past, the Quad Cities rediscovered its downtowns. "Reinvent" might be a better word. Between 1980 and 1990, each city developed civic organizations designed to bring the downtown back to life. These groups included Rejuvenate Davenport, Renew Moline, REDEEM East Moline, Rock Island's Development Association of Rock Island and its Downtown 2000 program. In the return to the downtown, Davenport made the first move. In 1982, the city began work on River Center, a 9 million-dollar convention and entertainment complex adjacent to a restored Black Hawk Hotel. That same year, the Davenport Chamber of Commerce bought the vacant Orpheum Theater building just to the west, and donated it to a non-profit corporation, River Center for the Performing Arts, for renovation. River Center opened on November 22, 1983. Three years later, the Orpheum Theater, restored through 4.2 million dollars in donations, one million of it from Lee Enterprises, opened as the 2,400 seat Adler Theater, named for two Davenport civic leaders, former presidents of Lee Enterprises, E. P. Adler and his son, Philip D. Adler. The construction of the River Center complex marked a gradual

turnaround in the flight from Davenport downtown. While old businesses continued to leave, new restaurants, stores, and businesses opened and others returned.

As was the case with Davenport, Moline's plans for its downtown reflected a shift from dependence on its former retail base to a service based economy. In January 1991, Moline broke ground in the central downtown for Superblock, a seven-story office building for 400 tenants. By the time it was completed in March 1992, the project, now called Heritage Place for its major tenant, Heritage National Healthplan, had already attracted a dozen new businesses to downtown Moline. Along the Moline waterfront near the site of the original John Deere plow factory, a 33.5 million-dollar Quad City Civic Center, the MARK, was completed in the spring of 1993.

Rock Island's role as the county seat and as the headquarters of three insurance companies kept its downtown alive; but it had lost more of a retailing base than either Moline or Davenport, and there was less agreement among city planners on how to fix it. A new Rock Island downtown happened more by accident than design. In the late 1980s, Rock Island found that it was becoming the center of an arts and entertainment district. Evolution of "The District," as the eastern section of the downtown was named late in 1991, began in 1978, when Dennis Hitchcock, against the prevailing local wisdom, opened a dinner theater, Circa 21, in the restored Fort Theater building. The success of Circa 21 served as a model

Courtesy, The President Riverboat Casino.

Photo by, P. Samuel Whitehead.

UPPER LEFT *RIVERBOAT GAMBLING CAME TO THE QUAD CITIES IN 1991. THE ARRIVAL OF THE BOATS AND TOURISTS BOOSTED BOTH MORALE AND SELF-IMAGE FOR QUAD CITIEANS WHO HOPED THE NEW LABEL OF "RIVERBOAT GAMBLING CAPITAL OF THE WORLD" WOULD BRING NEW POSSIBILI- TIES FOR THE FUTURE. THE PRESIDENT RIVERBOAT IS SHOWN ON THE MISSISSIPPI WITH THE CENTENNIAL BRIDGE IN THE BACKGROUND.*

LEFT *THIS BRONZE SCULPTOR OF ARTIST JOHN BLOOM'S "WATCHING THE FERRY" WAS DEDICATED IN THE SUMMER OF 1992. IT SITS ALONG THE RIVERFRONT IN EAST DAVENPORT. THE SCULPTOR SHOWS THE WIDE-EYED INNOCENCE OF YOUTH AND THE SIMPLE PLEASURES DERIVED FROM THE MISSIS- SIPPI RIVER.*

for other restoration projects and helped attract several new restaurants and night spots to the downtown. Hitchcock also opened The Speakeasy next door to Circa 21 to house the Comedy Sportz troupe and a mystery dinner-theater. In the summer of 1991, the Quad City Arts Council opened ArtsCenter, an office and gallery, in the old Block & Kuhl Department Store building. The Fort Armstrong Hotel, its lobby and ballroom restored to their original elegance, reopened as a living center for senior citizens in 1991. Buildings along the east side of the hotel have been razed for a new public park, named Spencer Square after the city's first park. In 1991, more than 24 projects were announced, begun, or completed as part of Rock Island's renewal.

The Quad Cities was already pointed toward recovery by the late 1980s when it received a boost from an unexpected source. After several years of attempts, the Iowa House and Senate both passed bills in 1989 legalizing riverboat gambling on the Mississippi and Missouri Rivers, subject to the local approval of river towns. In spite of strong opposition by the Coalition of Concerned Churches and Citizens, riverboat gambling was approved by 60% of Scott County voters in August of 1989.

Gambling arrived in the Iowa Quad Cities on April 1, 1991, amid waves of grand visions, plans and promises from two entrepreneurs. John Connelly's *The President*, operating from Davenport, and Bernard Goldstein's *Diamond Lady*, in Bettendorf, each began four gambling cruises a day. Although the extensive land-based developments that were to accompany the boats soon fell behind schedule, the boats themselves exceeded projections, helping to swell the number of tourists who spent at least one night in the Quad Cities in 1991 to 1,500,000. The smaller *Diamond Lady* had taken in $10,645,000 in gambling profits by the end of 1991, while the *President*'s profits reached $29,413,000 and the boat welcomed its millionth customer early in 1992.

Illinois passed its own version of riverboat gambling late in 1989. On March 11, 1992, the *Casino* *Rock* *Island* opened for business, joining the *President* and the *Diamond Lady* in making the Quad Cities the "Riverboat Gambling Capital of the World."

It is too soon to predict the long-term success of riverboat gambling—indeed, the first boat, the *Diamond Lady*, left Bettendorf in July 1992 for Biloxi, Mississippi—but the arrival of the boats and the tourists boosted both morale and self-image, and helped Quad Citians imagine new possibilities for the future.

As the Quad Cities maneuvers toward the 21st century, it carries important lessons from its rich history. From the example of the river itself, it has learned to expect and live with change. Neither river nor town nor business stands still; those businesses that have learned to adapt to new conditions always just around the next bend, are those that last. Davenport's Alter Company, for example, arose from a small cart in which two Russian immigrants, Morris and Harry Alter, began collecting scrap metal in the late 19th century. Growing as the times changed, the Alter Company's computerized scrap yard today goes through 300,000 cars, 250 million tons of aluminum cans, and a million tons of scrap steel a year. A shortage of barges in the 1950s led then president Frank Alter to establish a marine division for the company to haul its own scrap, resulting in a marine division with a fleet of towboats to haul others' goods as well. A son-in-law, Bernard Goldstein, joined the company in the 1950s and when riverboat gambling came to Iowa, established the Steamboat Development Corporation, owner of the *Diamond Lady*.

This ability to adapt is reflected in a number of Quad Cities institutions. Responding to the growing disparity between the sophisticated technological needs of the workplace and the lack of trained workers, Black Hawk and Scott community colleges have added services and programs nearly every year. The private colleges in the Quad Cities, faced with a declining number of high school graduates, each adapted in different ways as they had to earlier changes. Augustana dropped its masters level programs and set its goals on becoming a selective national liberal arts college. St. Ambrose moved in the opposite direction, expanding its range of courses to serving the needs of local communities with master's degrees in several business areas, became St. Ambrose University in 1988. In late 1990, Marycrest College merged with Teikyo University in Japan to become an American campus of that school, providing an American experience to a number of Japanese students.

A second lesson the Quad Cities has learned through past mistakes is the need for diversity. Often dependent in the past on a single industry, on steamboating, sawmilling, or the farm industry, the Quad Cities is determined not to repeat the mistake with riverboat gambling. Its vision for the future depends on variety. Both individual Quad Cities businesses and the range of those businesses show more diversity than ever. Deere and Company has grown from a small factory that made plows into a large conglomerate that today not only makes farm machinery, but markets lawn and garden equipment, sells insurance, and is currently planning to build its own health care facility in Moline in cooperation with the Mayo Clinic. The Rock Island Arsenal has also continued to expand from a manufacturer of military hardware into new commands and directions. Project REARM (Renovation of Armament Manufacturing) was transfered to the Arsenal in 1984, helping to boost local economy. Among other operations at the Arsenal today is one of the least known, but largest and most successful colleges in the Quad Cities. The Army Management and Engineering Training Agency was upgraded to a college in 1987, and yearly trains some 18,000 to 20,000 people in seminars and classes that range from three days to several weeks.

Although the Arsenal, Alcoa, and the remaining farm equipment factories continue to be the dominant industries, the Quad Cities' future increasingly rests on a variety of smaller operations, from those with one or two employees offering a single service, to newcomers like Nomura Enterprises, a technical writing service that moved to the Quad Cities in

1985 to be near its large customer, the Arsenal, to larger operations such as the 60 million-dollar Nichols-Homeshield plant in west Davenport, designed to manufacture aluminum products for the construction industry, which opened in 1991. The Quad Cities is increasing a center for high tech businesses such as Derby Tech and Unicor.

The third lesson has been the hardest: the need for all the disparate elements in the Quad Cities to cooperate. There are still many tentative trials and false starts. While Lutheran and Moline Public Hospitals merged to form United Medical Center in 1989, and subsequently with Franciscan Hospital in Rock Island to improve services and avoid duplication, other medical facilities continue to build competing centers. Mayors and city councils continue to berate their neighbors across town borders in an attempt to guard their own turf.

In spite of this posturing, the citizens themselves have little difficulty living in one city, shopping in a second, and entertaining themselves in a third. Aided by agencies such as the Bi-State Metropolitan Planning Commission and organizations such as the Quad City Chambers of Commerce Presidents, the many units that make up the Quad Cities have begun to plan together more than ever before. It is not likely that there will ever be one Quad City USA; previous attempts have all failed. Discussions in 1986 about merging the Illinois Quad Cities into one community ended after coming up with names such as Roline, Twain, and Missicities. But in spite of occasional squabbles, a few of them serious, each of the Quad Cities today knows that it cannot stand alone.

The difference cooperation can make is perhaps nowhere so apparent today as in the many organizations designed to ease conflicts between labor and management. In order to attract new businesses, both labor and management realized that they needed to change the reputation of the Quad Cities as a tough union town with a history of bitter strikes. Two organizations in the mid-1980s began to repair the damage: the Quad-City Area Labor-Management Council and, in 1986, the Illowa Construction Labor-Management Council. Illowa handles problems as they arise, especially on major construction projects, by having all sides reach an agreement to bring the project in on time, within budget, and with safe construction practices. In the past several years most major Quad Cities construction projects have been completed free of strikes. St. Ambrose University has added to its curriculum a Labor Management program, designed to train management and labor leaders to work together.

The Quad Cities is learning that lesson. If tourists are going to be attracted, and businesses encouraged to settle here, if the Quad Cities is going to be an urban area with the services of a large metropolis, each city will have to cooperate, contributing its own strengths to the mosaic along the river.

Epilogue

AND THEN THE RAINS CAME. IN MAY OF 1993, AMID ALL THE DOWNTOWN RENEWAL PROJECTS, THE MISSISSIPPI RIVER UNEXPECTEDLY ASSERTED its power. Torrential and continued rains along much of the Upper Mississippi Valley—a record 13.62 inches during June in the Quad Cities—pushed the Mississipppi and its tributaries above the flood stage by the middle of June. As the rains continued, the first optimistic crest estimates had to be revised up and up. By the first week in July the Quad Cities had become a national media event, worthy of a visit by President Clinton and meriting major coverage abroad as well. Still, the rains came—thirty-eight straight days.

At 4 a.m. on July 9, the Mississippi River crested at 22.63 feet in the Quad Cities, eclipsing the 1965 crest of 22.48 feet. The great Flood of '93, as it came to be called, hit Davenport's unprotected downtown expecially hard, flooding out businesses all along River Drive. Rock Island's levee saved it from much of the damage. Residents along the Rock River were especially hard hit as the flood created six separate crests from April through July.

The water sank slowly all during July, leaving behind a trail of mud, ruined homes and businesses, and buckled streets. On August 1, the Mississippi fell below flood stage for the first time since June 21. Quad Citians began the process of rebuilding.

Though bricks and mortar collapsed, spirits of Quad Citians remained high; perhaps people were even prouder of their rich heritage which owed so much to the river. Abandoned to time and the elements for more than a hundred years, the Davenport House along the north shore of Arsenal Island is today being carefully restored to its original grandeur. The main house looks today much as it did in the 1830s.

Standing on the front porch of this house, in which so many of the plans and plattings were hatched that grew into cities, businesses, and railroads, one can view the results of those schemes. At the edge of the front lawn lies the Mississippi River which originally brought both Indians and whites to this area. Marquette and Joliet passed this way in June of 1673, Zebulon Pike and Stephen Long came here exploring. Somewhere in the river near the

Davenport House is the site of Robert E. Lee's impromptu office on a wrecked steamboat in the rapids. The *Virginia*, the *Effie Afton*, the *Grey Eagle*, and the long strings of the log rafts are gone, the Rock Island Rapids has disappeared under a pool of water from Lock and Dam 15 downstream, but the river is busier than ever at human affairs. On a warm summer evening, performing for an audience of people fishing, walking, biking or just watching from both sides of the river, towboats with their loads of barges slowly maneuver into line for Lock 15. Some 30,000 of those barges, in tows of up to 17 at a time, passed by the Quad Cities in 1991. Any single barge could carry the 1823 *Virginia* comfortably. Gambling boats, lights blazing, recreate 19th century designs as they appear in the distance and swing back upstream during a dinner cruise. Pleasure craft dot the water surface, from small open boats to large cruisers and sailing boats.

Just downstream from the Davenport House stand the bridges which ended the steamboat monopoly. The first bridge is gone, but a memorial pier marks its location west of the house. Its replacement, the Government Bridge, crosses the river futher downstream. Just visible in the distance are the arches of the 1941 Centennial Bridge.

Across the river itself lies the Marguerite LeClaire reserve, site of a Mesquakie village and of the treaty signing ending the 1832 Black Hawk War. On the bluffs above the river stands the LeClaire Mansion, followed by blocks of homes and businesses whose mosaic of architectures illustrates the history of the Quad Cities. Just visible upstream is the Village of East Davenport, one of the sawmilling centers on the Mississippi and the site of Camp McClellan.

Around the Davenport House on the island itself, one can see evidence of the military presence which has been part of Quad City history from the beginning. To the west rises the Clock Tower Building out of which grew General Rodman's Rock Island Arsenal visible to the east. Much more of what began in the Davenport House lies hidden behind the island to the south. Here, in Illinois, smaller bluffs and more modest architecture mirror the story told by the Iowa side.

Only from the air today could one sense the full impact of what began in the Davenport House. George Davenport and Antoine LeClaire were

Courtesy, The Dispatch/The Rock Island Argus

Courtesy, The Dispatch/The Rock Island Argus.

followed by a host of city planners, of schemers and dreamers, of movers and drifters, of men and women all subject to the accidents and fortunes of history, who played some part in creating the mosaic known as the Quad Cities. From the air, one could see many of the individual pieces of that mosaic that contribute to the quality of life for the people living there. Prominent would be the industries and businesses which support a labor force of some 186,000, and the stores clustered in five downtown business districts and twenty-one shopping centers. Visible also would be those pieces of the mosaic that enrich the lives of the people: the 302 churches, cathedrals, and synagogues, seven hospitals, 125 private and public schools and colleges, 17 golf courses, and 80 parks.

Even from the air, however, one could not see the richest asset of the Quad Cities, the people who live in the individual pieces of mosaic and make the whole picture work. They are a mosaic themselves: an ethnic mosaic of Germans, Irish, and Swedes who came in the 1840s and 50s, of Belgians, Greeks, and Eastern Europeans who came in the 1890s, of Blacks and Mexicans who came after the turn of the century, of the Chinese and Native Americans of the 1960s, and the Asian Indians, Laotians, and Vietnamese who began arriving in the 1970s. Quad Citians are a mosaic, too, of interests and abilities. Many of them belong to one or more of the 450 Quad Cities civic organizations or serve at one of the more than 140 social service agencies working to make life better.

Immigrants are still arriving in the Quad Cities, though they are more likely to come from Minneapolis or Des Moines today than from Vermont or Germany. What they discover when they get here is a frontier as demanding as that which faced Davenport and LeClaire. Overhead may have replaced grasshoppers as the enemy, but each new business, each new job, is a frontier of opportunities and risks.

It is this frontier spirit which the Quad Cities recaptured in the 1980s. The values and skills which the first settlers brought with them are the same tools needed today as the Quad Cities faces the 21st century. There is as much need as ever for the entrepreneur, for new John Deeres, new Velies, Bettendorfs, and Al Tunicks, who imagine the almost impossible. There is a need for corporate and business leaders, men and women like Charles Deere, the Butterworths, the Hewitts, Geraldine Towner of Royal Neighbors, and Davenport's Figges and Adlers, wise and faithful servants to businesses large and small.

Above all, the Quad Cities needs its thousands of solid citizens who, like Annie Wittenmyer and Phebe Sudlow, believe they can leave their community better than they found it—the teachers, householders, bakers, library aides, clerks, and factory workers who attend PTA, serve on city councils, cook pork sandwiches for the Rotary booth or pancakes for the Kiwanis breakfasts, who spend Saturdays with Breachmenders restoring houses or serve a meal at the Salvation Army. These are people of vision like Marion Lardner, who cut a hole in a fence separating Earl Hanson School in Rock Island from a retarded shelter so that the shelter people could join her kindergarteners in the joy of planting and tending a garden, or like Davenport's Sandra Lake-Bullock, once homeless, who got back on her feet and now spends her time turning houses she aquires into homeless shelters. Still others like John and Susanne Hauberg, Mel McKay, and Doris and Victor Day left legacies that have kept making the Quad Cities better long after they were gone.

It is this amazing mosaic of Quad Citians, more than new civic centers, gambling boats, and renewed downtowns, who are responsible for this east-west bend in the Mississippi "looking better every day."

On their wings, the Quad Cities is truly "soaring ahead."

Quad City Enterprises

As originally envisioned, this book was to have a section featuring local firms and institutions, with biographical sketches and photos of each. Windsor Publications of California, a well-rated publisher of community histories, contracted to organize the project with local sponsorship by the Quad City Heritage League. Windsor solicited the local companies and for their participation they were to receive biographical entries in the book. Unfortunately, Windsor's subsequent bankruptcy and dissolution necessitated cancellation of that portion of the project. We wish to thank those enterprises for their faith in the Quad City Heritage League and their understanding of the turn the original project has taken. The original participating enterprises are listed by their current corporate titles:

American Honda Motor Co., Inc.
2015 West Lake Boulevard
Davenport, IA 52804

American Institute of Commerce
1801 East Kimberly Road
Davenport, IA 52807

The Blackhawk Hotel
Davenport, IA 52801

Davenport Electric Contract Company
529 Pershing Avenue
Davenport, IA 52803
Fredrick D. Fuessel, President

Deere and Company
Moline, IL 61265

Eagle Food Centers
Rock Island, IL 61204-6700

Genesis Health System
Offering Comprehensive, Regional Healthcare Services
1227 East Rusholme Street
Davenport, IA 52803
(319) 326-6512

Group O Company
P.O. Box 170
Milan, IL 61264

Hansaloy Corporation
820 West 35th Street
Davenport, IA 52806

Heeren Company
513 31st Avenue
Rock Island, IL 61201

Iowa-American Water Company
230 East Second Street
Davenport, IA 52801

Jaydon Inc.
Rock Island, IL 61201

KWQC-TV 6
805 Brady Street
Davenport, IA 52803

McGladrey & Pullen
Des Moines, IA 50309-2372

McLaughlin Body Company
J.T. McLaughlin
R.L. McLaughlin

MidAmerican Energy Company
Davenport, IA 52801

Moline Forge, Inc.
Moline, IL 61265

Montgomery Kone
Moline, IL 61265

Nichols-Homeshield
210 West Second Street
Suite 420
Davenport, IA 52801

Northwest Bank and Trust Company
Davenport, IA 52806

Palmer College of Chiropractic
1000 Brady Street
Davenport, IA 52803
Dr. Virgil Strang, President

Plaza One Hotel
One Plaza Square
Rock Island, IL 61201

The President Riverboat Casino
212 Brady Street
Davenport, IA 52801
(319) 328-8000

Quad City Times
Davenport, IA 52801

Royal Neighbors of America
National Headquarters,
Rock Island, IL
Grandview Terrace, National Home
Davenport, IA

St. Ambrose University
518 West Locust Street
Davenport, IA 52803
(319) 333-6000

Stern Beverage, Inc.
1005 West Eleventh Street
Milan, IL 61264
Michael J. Stern—President
Roanald J. Heinzman—Vice-President

Story Construction Company
100 East Kimberly Road
Davenport, IA 52806

Teikyo Marycrest University
"Developing citizens for the world through education
without prejudice"
1607 West Twelfth Street
Davenport, IA 52804

Tri-City Electric Company
Davenport, IA 52801

Trinity Medical Center
Rock Island and Moline, IL

Uticor Technology Inc.
Bettendorf, IA 52722

Whitey's Ice Cream Stores

Williams, White and Company
Moline, IL 61265

WQAD TV 8
Moline, IL
61265

WQPT-TV Public Television
Moline, IL 61265

A List of Sources

Anderson, Frederick I, Ed. *Joined By a River Quad Cities*. [Davenport, IA]: Lee Enterprises, 1982.

Bateman, Newton, and Paul Selby. *Historical Encyclopedia of Illinois and History of Rock Island County*. 2 vols. Chicago: Munsell Publishing Co., 1914.

Beltrami, J. C. *A Pilgrimage in Europe and America, Leading to the Discovery of the Source of the Mississippi and Bloody River*. 2 vols. London: Hunt and Clark, 1828.

Bouilly, Robert H., and Thomas J. Slattery. *Rock Island Arsenal: A Historical Tour Guide with Photographs & Narrative*. [Rock Island, IL]: Armcom Historical Office, n.d.

Bowers, Martha H., and Marlys Svendsen. *Davenport Architecture: Tradition and Transition*. [Davenport: City of Davenport, 1984].

Broehl, Wayne G., Jr. *John Deere's Company, a History of Deere & Company and Its Times*. New York: Doubleday, 1984.

Burghardt, Andrew F. "The Location of River Towns in the Central Lowlands of the United States." *Annals of the Association of American Geographers* 49 (1959): 305-323.

Downer, Harry E. *Early Davenport*. [Davenport: Friendly House, 1931]

_____, *History of Davenport and Scott County Iowa*. 2 vols. Chicago: S. J. Clarke, 1910.

Economic Development Strategy for the Inner City Area of the Quad City Metropolitan Area. [Rock Island, IL]: Bi-State Metropolitan Planning Commission, 1979.

Elsner, B. J., ed. *Rock Island: Yesterday, Today & Tomorrow*. Rock Island: Rock Island County History Book Committee, 1988.

England, Otis Bryan. *A Short History of the Rock Island Barracks,* Revised Edition. Rock Island, IL: Historical Office, U. S. Army Armament, Munitions, & Chemical Compound Command, 1985.

Espenshade, Edward B., Jr. *Urban Development at the Upper Rapids of the Mississippi*. Diss. U. of Chicago, 1944. Chicago: Edward B. Espenshade, Jr., 1944.

Ficke, Charles August. *Memories of Fourscore Years*. Davenport, IA: Graphic Services, 1930.

Fleishaker, Oscar. *The Iowa-Illinois Jewish Community on the Banks of the Mississippi River*. Diss. Yeshiva U., 1957.

Fulton, Ambrose C. *A Life's Voyage, A Diary of a Sailor on Sea and Land*. New York: Published by the author, 1898.

Groskopf, Amy, and Kermit Westerberg, eds. *Quad City Heritage Source Guide: A Guide to Quad City Area Organizations Dedicated to Preserving the History and Heritage of the Quad Cities*. [Moline, IL]: Quad City Heritage League, 1991.

Hartsough, Mildred L. *From Canoe to Steel Barge on the Upper Mississippi*. Minneapolis: University of Minnesota Press, 1934.

Hero Street, U. S. A. Videorecording. [St. Louis, MO]: Busch Creative Services Corporation, 1984.

Historic Rock Island County. Rock Island: Kramer & Co., 1908.

History of Scott County, Iowa. Chicago: Interstate Publishing Company, 1882.

Johnson, Hildegard Binder. *Order Upon the Land*. New York: Oxford, 1976.

Lage, Dorothy. *LeClaire, Iowa. A Mississippi River Town*. Davenport: Dorothy Lage, 1976.

Lardner, Peter. *The Germans and the Greeks: A Comparative Study of Ethnic Assimilation in the Quad-Cities*. M.A. thesis, Augustana College, 1982.

McMaster, S. W. *Sixty Years on the Upper Mississippi, My Life and Experiences*. Rock Island: n.p., 1893.

Moline Plan Commission. *The Economic Potential of the Davenport-Rock Island-Moline Metropolitan Area: A First Report*. Moline: City of Moline, 1965.

Oszuscik, Philippe. *Nineteenth Century Architectural Development in the Upper Mississippi Valley: Davenport, Rock Island and Moline*. [Davenport]: Putnam Museum, 1981.

Our Story: Bridging the Past and the Present. [LeClaire, IA: Sesquicentennial History Book Committee, 1984.]

Past and Present of Rock Island County, Ill. Chicago: H. F. Kett, 1877.

Peck, J[ohn] M[ason]. *A Guide for Emigrants, Containing Sketches of Illinois, Missouri, and the Adjacent Parts*. Boston: Lincoln & Edmands, 1831.

Petersen, William J. *Steamboating on the Upper Mississippi*. Iowa City, IA: State Historical Society of Iowa, 1968.

Pierce, Bess. *Moline A Pictorial History*. Virginia Beach, VA: Donning Co., 1981.

Portrait and Biographical Album of Rock Island County, Illinois. Chicago: Biographical Publishing Company, 1885.

Rabin, Jonathan. *Old Glory An American Voyage*. New York: Simon & Schuster, 1981.

Roba, William. *The River and the Prairie: A History of the Quad-Cities*. Davenport, IA: Hesperian Press, 1986.

Russell, Charles Edward. *A-Rafting on the Mississippi*. New York: Century Co., 1928.

Schick, Joseph S. *The Early Theater in Eastern Iowa, Cultural Beginnings and the Rise of Theater in Davenport & Eastern Iowa 1836-1863*. Chicago: University of Chicago Press, 1939.

Scott, Barbara, and Virginia Anderson. *Travels in Time Milan, Illinois*. Mediapolis, IA: New Era Print, 1982.

Shovar, Mary, ed. *Home on the River . . . in Andalusia, Illinois*. Davenport, IA: Moore Printing Co., 1983.

Slattery, Thomas J. *An Illustrated History of the Rock Island Arsenal and Arsenal Island*. Revised Edition. Rock Island, IL: Historical Office, U. S. 7Armament Command, 1990.

Spenser, J. W., and J. M. D. Burrows. *The Early Days of Rock Island and Davenport*. Chicago: Lakeside Press, 1942.

Strategic Plan and Implementation; Together We Can Make It Happen. Rock Island, IL: Quad Cities Vision for the Future, 1989.

Svendsen, Marlys. *Davenport, a Pictorial History 1836-1986*. [S.l.]: City of Davenport, 1982.

————, *Davenport Historical Survey Report*. [Davenport: City of Davenport], 1980.

————, *Davenport, Where the Mississippi Runs West*. Davenport: City of Davenport, 1982.

Tillinghast, Benjamin Franklin. *Three Cities: Davenport, Rock Island, and Moline: Their Location, Industrial Enterprise*. Davenport: Egbert, Fidlar & Chambers, 1888.

Turner, Frederick Jackson. *The United States 1830-1850, The Nation and Its Sections*. New York: Peter Smith, 1950.

Tweet, Roald. *A History of the Rock Island District U. S. Army Corps of Engineers 1866-1983*. Rock Island: U. S. ArmyEngineer District, Rock Island, 1984.

————. *History of Transportation on the Upper Mississippi and Illinois Rivers*. National Waterways Study. [Ft, Belvoir, VA]: Institute for Water Resources, 1983.

Voelliger, Arthur J., and Dorothy Lage. *History of Bettendorf and Pleasant Valley*. [Bettendorf, IA]: Bettendorf Public Library, 1973.

War's Greatest Workshop, Rock Island Arsenal: Historical, Topographical and Illustrative. [Rock Island, IL]: Arsenal Publishing Company of the Tri-Cities, 1922.

Wilkie, Franc B. *Davenport Past and Present*. Davenport: Luse, Lane & Co., 1858.

Wissler, Clark. *Indians of the U. S.* New York: Doubleday, 1966.

Other Sources:

Much of the primary material, as well as additional secondary material, for this volume came from three local newspapers, the *Moline Dispatch*, the *Quad-City Times*, and the *Rock Island Argus*, as well as their many predecessors. I have also made extensive use of the historical archives of the Davenport, Moline, and Rock Island public libraries, as well as the archives of the Augustana College Library (especially the Davenport Papers and the Hauberg Collections), the Arsenal Historical Office, the Rock Island County Historical Society, and the Putnam Museum.

Index